## PRACTICAL ADVICE
### FROM A FUNERAL & FINANCIAL INSIDER

## GREG BARNSDALE

Certified Executor Advisor
Certified Financial Planner
Licensed Funeral Director

The following information is intended as a general reference tool to help understand the underlying principles and practices of the subject matter covered. The opinions and ideas expressed herein are solely those of the author. The author and publisher are not engaged in rendering financial, estate or legal advice. The publication is not intended to provide a basis for action in particular circumstances without consideration by a competently appropriate professional.

◆ FriesenPress

One Printers Way
Altona, MB R0G 0B0
Canada

www.friesenpress.com

**Copyright © 2023 by Greg Barnsdale**
First Edition — 2023

ISBN
978-1-5255-8491-6 (Hardcover)
978-1-5255-8490-9 (Paperback)
978-1-5255-8492-3 (eBook)

*1. Business & Economics, Personal Finance, Retirement Planning*

Distributed to the trade by The Ingram Book Company

Attention: Quantity discounts are available to your company, educational institution or writing organization for reselling, educational purposes, subscription incentives, gifts or fundraiser campaigns. Our discount schedule is aggressive. Please contact us using one of the methods below;

www.DoNotIgnoreYourMortality.com
sales@DoNotIgnoreYourMortality.com

*To all the dead people I have met over my career.*
*I am sure many of you did not have your affairs in order.*
*The endless stories I have heard and overheard*
*from your grieving relatives and friends*
*clarify that many sour situations like yours*
*could have been avoided.*
*This has pushed me to the point of taking this bold stand.*
*My commitment to all of you*
*is to inspire many others to have their affairs organized.*
*We both know the lingering regrets of not being prepared*
*last an awfully long time.*

# INTRODUCTION

*I*n my career of more than 30 years, I have been surrounded by death and end-of-life roles. I have witnessed the worst circumstances countless times. I have also seen how proactive foresight and thoughtful planning have left positive, loving memories for survivors. This is the legacy all of us need to leave behind.

Death is a situation that no one can be entirely prepared for. Most people do not have the experience with the issues surrounding death to be familiar with it. I hope to help improve that by clarifying some of the uncertainty.

This book is different from many others. It has been written from the perspective of a quiet-natured fellow, with firsthand experience in planning ahead correctly, taking several points of view. I address issues of avoidance and control, which for many people is a struggle (myself included). I hope my experience will help you and those you love and care about.

My objective is to help reduce your stress, provide practical methods to save your family money, help enhance relationships, and inspire you to leave a memorable legacy. Each of us will leave some sort of legacy when we die but leaving the best one possible is my message. Too many people close their minds to the concept of dramatic changes occurring in their life. Lottery winners are rare; death is inevitable.

It is happening all around us, all the time. Unfortunately, however, many people are literally tuned out. Even though we are increasingly exposed to death on the news and online, far too many have the perspective of 'it won't happen to me' mentality. Others do not know where to begin. This is not only a significant problem in North America but on several other continents as well.

The emotional toll death has on survivors is often intense, long-lasting, and real. It is the universal humanizing condition to which none of us are immune. Society would be much better off embracing their mortality and controlling what they can, while they can.

When we are young adults, we are eager to make our own decisions. It is a natural progression of becoming an independent adult. The control we have is prevalent throughout our lives, and we do not want it taken from us. Does it, therefore, also make sense that we should do our best to control what happens after we die? To a degree, this is indeed possible.

My experiences have allowed me to conclude that the key to dramatically eliminating the familiar feelings of frustration and regret after a death can be successfully achieved by preparing for what we want to have happen before it occurs. Aside from an unexpected accident, we do have that control.

As responsible adults, we pride ourselves on building a life with purpose and meaning. Raising our children to be successful members of society and helping them achieve their goals is the objective for many of us. As a responsible parent, it is the right thing to do. Is it not also our responsibility to plan for the end of our own lives, to ultimately make it easier for those we love? Yes, it is.

Think of the following five chapters as your key to communicating and planning your wishes for the essential phase of your life – the last one. It takes courage to face your mortality, and it takes focused action to put prudent strategies into place. Your reward will be less stress, stronger relationships, and greater peace of mind.

There is no need for your final moments to be filled with worry and regret. Having your affairs in order is one of the most unique gifts of love you can give. This nurturing process fills you with a calm that will permeate every aspect of your remaining life. With so many benefits to making your final plans, there are no reasons to postpone it.

My message will remind you of the delicate nature of life. It will help you better understand the significance of being adequately prepared and how to effectively move that vital process forward. Below is a brief description of what is to follow.

- Chapter 1 discusses the importance of communication, what a lack of it can cause and how to ensure your final wishes are respected.

- Chapter 2 examines the topic of wills, types, and how to set them up.

- Chapter 3 discusses funeral, cremation, and burial planning.

- Chapter 4 addresses overall estate/legacy planning.

- Chapter 5 examines powers of attorney/personal directives.

The Summary provides inspiration to help you with this important planning. It also touches on how the stress of growing older can actually be reduced by going through this process.

As you read through the chapters, I suggest that you take notes for future reference.

Let us begin.

# TABLE OF CONTENTS

# *1*

# COMMUNICATION IS KEY

Openly sharing your end of life wishes with your loved ones will provide direction and comfort in difficult times

*"If you would not be forgotten as soon as you are dead, either write something worth reading or do something worth writing."*

—BENJAMIN FRANKLIN

*L*et me start by sincerely congratulating you. Reading information about the end of your life is not easy. Taking the proper steps to plan for it is not easy either, but you will feel much better as a result. Your family will certainly appreciate it. Others will also.

I completely understand the reluctance most people have when discussing (or even considering) the end of their lives. We often live our lives assuming each day will continue similarly to the previous day. It is difficult for many people to envision their body shutting down permanently, but I can assure you that at some point, your body will shut down regardless of the plans you had scheduled.

Death affects us all, and even though I have worked in the funeral industry for years, I am not immune to the same feelings and fears as anyone else. As I get older, I think about my life and its limitations more often. It seems natural to do so.

It is not my intention to weigh you down with a gloomy perspective. I certainly respect the delicate nature of life and try hard to be grateful for each day I am blessed to have. It's so easy to get caught up in the day-to-day things, but it is essential we maintain a proper perspective. As you read this, remember that many people did not survive yesterday, and many others will not get through today. As one of the great philosophers of all time, Marcus Aurelius so well stated almost 2000 years ago, "When you awake in the morning, think of the precious privilege it is to be alive, to breathe, to think, to enjoy, to love." Like many other things, this awareness is easy to take for granted. (I am certainly guilty of it, at least occasionally).

Statistics surrounding our mortality are significant, and the number of deaths is increasing. Approximately 300,000 people in Canada die each year[1], and about 3 million people die in the United States annually.[2] Granted, the population of Canada is almost 40 million, and that of the United States is over 330 million[3] the number of people dying regularly is substantial. The Covid-19 pandemic increased the mortality rate and heightened awareness surrounding the importance of estate planning. That appreciation, however, will not likely result in much improvement regarding the reality of being prepared. Considering the far-reaching statistics below, a shift in thinking about mortality is long overdue—a healthier, more accepting change.

Less than half of the Canadian adult population has a current and valid will[4], and fewer Americans are prepared in this way.[5] Despite all the extensive efforts of the legal, financial, and funeral industries stressing the benefits of proper estate planning for decades, most people do not 'have their affairs in order.' When a death occurs, far too many people are left struggling with decisions and issues that should have been resolved before the death took place – and government involvement could have been mostly avoided. I have witnessed this frustratingly unfortunate situation so many times that it makes my body chemistry change as I write this.

DO NOT IGNORE YOUR MORTALITY

The dilemma is common in other countries as well. Two Australian universities (in conjunction with the Society of Trust and Estate Practitioners) completed an extensive report on this very topic. The detailed research concluded: "In summary, our results indicate the 'it will never happen to me' mentality is alive and well. Clearly, there is a need for people to be more adequately prepared for end-of-life events and incapacity".[6]

The United Kingdom has a similar problem with their population also suffering from inaction.[7] China does as well, and to a much larger degree. Very few of this massive country's citizens have prepared estate plans, primarily due to superstition. China's cultural roots view such topics as taboo and writing a will to be perceived as putting a curse on oneself. Their Court system is struggling with the resulting inheritance disputes as many families are turning against each other.[8]

An increasing number of people realize the importance of this. However, there is still a significant gap between those good intentions of getting organized and following through effectively. A growing amount of research reveals that many people simply do not know where to start the process.[9] As a result, this vital task is easily put off, and the statistics confirm the planning often never takes place. This issue is significant and desperately needs to improve for many reasons. It negatively affects millions of families on several continents, drains valuable Court resources, and destroys otherwise beautiful legacies. It could be the largest 'elephant in the room' we face.

As I was revising this manuscript, my home province of Ontario, Canada, announced an unprecedented investment of 72 million dollars into our Court system.[10] The Covid-19 pandemic caused our already over-burdened structure to fall much further behind. Inspiring more people to have a current and valid will in place is certainly worthwhile, as Ontario is not alone with this problem.

I want to help improve these issues through education and inspiration. The following pages will show you how to be prepared and make the process easier. It begins with communication.

First, the definition of 'estate planning' itself needs to change. According to the Merriam-Webster dictionary, the legal definition of estate planning is described as "The arranging for the disposition and management of one's estate at death through the use of wills, trusts, insurance policies, and other devices."[11] The word estate typically relates to death. This rather cold definition should be updated to be more inclusive of our relationships with those we love. This would make a significant difference.

Unfortunately, the theme of estate planning has taken on a predominately financial focus. It's not about our money; it is more about harmony. When people are dying, it is those they love and hold dear who they want nearby. It is not their money or prized possessions that give them comfort in their final hours. The strength of our relationships is vital, and this is primarily the result of effective and open communication.

With that point in mind, I suggest the term estate planning be replaced with 'legacy planning.' Everyone leaves some sort of legacy footprint when they are gone. Whether yours is basic or elaborate, you will leave a footprint. This reminder of your legacy surviving you is inspiring and hopeful. It is the impact you have made on others that outlives you. If society can embrace a more optimistic attitude about mortality, more people will be inclined to plan ahead.

It is your responsibility to let others know what you want to happen after you die – regardless of your bank account size or situation. This chapter will help you to discuss your wishes with those you love. The second chapter will discuss how to effectively make sure your wishes are honored and make it much easier for those who survive you.

When I worked as a funeral director, the frequent conversations surrounding death with surviving family members were essential (not a tremendous insight, I know). The reason they came to the funeral home was to discuss and arrange for their deceased loved one's cremation or burial. The conversation was entirely different when I worked as a financial planner. In this role, I was required to discuss potential roadblocks to the client's retirement objectives, and a major one was premature death. Some clients did not want to discuss such things. It made them uncomfortable. Being one of the few financial planners who was also a funeral director, I was keen to share my insights. Several, however, were open to the idea and agreed to a detailed analysis of the financial impact a death would cause. Clients and I frequently discovered they were underinsured and should consider buying life insurance or more of it.

The conversations I had with my financial planning clients about the impact of a potential death, was for many of them, the first time they had discussed this with a planner. My view toward the risk of death was genuine, unlike most other financial planners I had met or have yet to meet. Undertakers who also sell life insurance can't help but have a unique perspective toward mortality. It was indeed a distinct advantage when I worked as a financial planner.

Many of us have heard of situations where sudden death has occurred. The community rallies together with a fund-raising campaign to assist the immediate family struggling financially. Cases involving the support of young children come to mind. These are often instances where communication and proactive planning would have made a big difference in creating greater security for those survivors.

The reality is many people simply do not have enough insurance to provide adequate support for their family if death were to strike (or if a critical illness or disability should occur, for that matter).[12] This is a profoundly serious issue that many more people need to consider and ultimately do something about. Investing in good quality life insurance can be cost-effective and relatively easy. I have spoken with many people who regret not having this coverage in place when it was needed. Good insurance is like a parachute; it seems of little value until you need it.

After working as a financial planner for several years, I took the unusual step of establishing a unique end-of-life-focused insurance business within a large funeral home. I wanted to determine if the theme and location of my approach would make a positive difference in people's openness to discuss these issues. It did to a small degree, but some clients refused to come to my office at the funeral home. It made them uneasy. I must admit, though, having clients witness the typical public activities within a funeral home did prove to successfully open their minds to have an assessment of their life insurance needs completed.

I have been fortunate to have helped many people be better prepared by providing guidance in pre-need funeral planning, creating greater financial security after a death, reducing estate costs, arranging for private asset transfers at death, and discussing the generalities of wills and powers of attorney. Many of those I've helped have indicated a great sense of relief, with some even stating they had wanted to be organized in this way for years.

Considering the prevalence of second/third marriages, more complex end-of-life regulations, aging demographics, and the increasing risk of premature death, being adequately prepared is certainly responsible. The unnecessary frustration, anguish, additional time, wasted money, and destroyed legacies can be eliminated mainly by open dialogue and appropriate planning long before a death occurs. I have seen the positive results of this thoughtful planning firsthand, resulting in less stress, increased peace of mind, and ultimately, a healthier grieving experience for survivors.

The general reluctance to plan ahead has slowly been improving with a growing number of people becoming engaged. However, statistics confirm there are still significant gaps in planning for many. The funeral industry is not alone in its marketing efforts of stressing the benefits. The financial planning industry and legal industry are also prominent advocates of this important topic, and rightly so. They often discuss these issues with their clients as part of a well-rounded approach to providing the best advice. There is a growing collaboration between professional advisors from various industries to assist clients. It has been inspiring to witness these professionals' integrated approaches for the common good.

It is in everyone's best interest to be at least somewhat familiar with these things. The topic can seem overwhelming, but a basic understanding of the process and the rules will make a significant difference in your comfort level. You may be asked to look after someone's affairs and become a decision-maker on their behalf. (The formal name for this role is 'executor,' but it is also known as an estate trustee, fiduciary, or liquidator). You may instead be asked to be part of a team of executors, along with other relatives. If so, you will likely feel honored to be asked. Many people accept the invitation as if they have been asked to be the best man for a friend's wedding. However, the reality of being an executor comes with serious responsibilities and high potential risk. These are discussed in detail in Chapter Four. A female executor is known as an executrix. I will take a gender-neutral approach and simply use the traditional term executor.

Far too many people do not understand what happens after a death. Here is the simple truth. When no planning has taken place in advance, it is harder for your family in several ways. Without clear instruction, they will not know what you want them to do or who is to do what. You will be forcing them to deal with many unfamiliar challenges, mainly due to government involvement. You may be setting up your loved ones to fight among themselves, pay more of your money to the government and cause bitter memories which could have been avoided by completing your planning while you were alive. It will likely be a highly emotional time too. A well-organized estate can take 12 months or longer to settle all the details.[13] On the other hand, an unorganized mess can take much longer to finalize and creates numerous problems.

A Court of law is usually involved after a death, whether the deceased had a will in place or not. If you die without a valid will (also known as dying intestate), the government will decide how your assets are dispersed. If there is no one to leave your assets to, the government keeps them (in some jurisdictions). Even if you have a particular person in mind to be your executor, there is certainly no guarantee he/she will be your executor after your death. Intestate situations require government rules to take over. Someone from your family may apply to the Court to be your executor, but the role may be filled by someone else. It will not be as smooth a process compared to you having a valid will in the first place.

The time to communicate your end-of-life wishes with those you love is long before anything happens, which would make it difficult or impossible to have the conversations (yes, I know, another tremendous insight). I have spent substantial amounts of time with many survivors who are almost consumed with anxiety and regret as they realize these meaningful conversations never took place, and proper planning was never completed. Is that heavy burden, something you really want to force on those you love? Especially when you are no longer here to provide emotional support? I can feel my body chemistry changing again.

When people are forced to discuss these emotionally charged topics at the time of a death or a serious health dilemma, it is simply much more difficult. Traveling back to when the deceased was alive is not an option. Similar problems occur when someone is hospitalized and cannot make their own decisions. Asking your loved one if they prefer a wood or metal casket while looking back at you from a hospital bed is not a conversation, I suggest you initiate. Having to ask someone you care about if they have their will and power of attorney documents in place is not easy either, at such a time. Yet these types of sensitive conversations are forced upon family members frequently.

In these situations, we do want to remain optimistic, right? When a loved one is hospitalized, we provide uplifting messages of love and support but trying to bring up these end-of-life issues is almost perceived as taboo. This is the worst time to have these discussions because they are then forced, uncomfortable, and highly sensitive. The best time to discuss these topics is when things are normal, health is stable, minds are clear, and time is plentiful.

When my relatively active 82-year-old mother fell and broke her hip, I reassured her with the typical responses that most of us have used. "You'll be fine, mom. You're getting the best care. Get some rest, and you'll be home with dad soon". Little did I know she would flat line in front of me the next morning in the hospital, promptly end up on life support, and die the following morning. It seemed like a bad dream. I don't know if I could have brought up the issues with her about end-of-life planning while at her bedside. It would have broken my heart. Looking back, I am grateful that she was willing to discuss and get her affairs in order long before they were needed.

I am confident that as you read this, you are likely thinking of your particular situation. If you are not, you should be. Have you had 'the talk'? Would your survivors know what you want to happen if you died last night? Or who is to do what? Don't be overwhelmed by these things.

Be grateful you can still have these meaningful legacy conversations with those you love. For example, letting your spouse know where you keep your computer login credentials recorded is crucial. An increasing amount of our lives now require passwords.

I recall speaking with an accountant who was assisting a client whose spouse had died suddenly. She told me the surviving husband was extremely distraught and exhausted because his deceased wife had not made it easy for anyone to know her computer passwords. This complicated his grief and dramatically affected this poor husband, who was coping with a massive loss and caring for his young children by himself. Letting someone close to you know where you record your online passwords is relatively easy but too often overlooked.

Working as an undertaker, you witness many things. I recall several situations where relieved family members would say things like, "Grandma was always so thoughtful. She had her funeral all planned and prepaid. She was organized and had everything in order". It was a refreshing conversation instead of the more common scenario based in anguish, regret, and worry. In the former type of situation, the deceased had accepted the fact she was not going to live forever and planned accordingly. Effective planning helps to ensure your final wishes will be carried out the way you want them to be. How satisfying is that? We know that our absence will be felt by those we love, yet all we need to do is plan. Our ultimate exit will therefore be easier.

As I was writing this book, I had a jolting reminder of my own mortality. I came close to being killed in a car wreck. If the timing had been slightly different, I would have become another traffic fatality statistic. Even though the vehicle I was driving at the time was written off as a 'total loss,' I was extremely fortunate to walk away with no significant injuries. The other driver was charged with breaking the law. My wife has since asked me a few times if all my affairs are really in order. Fortunately, they are, as I am regularly communicating such things to those closest to me, but I do have some updating to do. I'll get around to it. (Just kidding).

The modern realities of our society create further challenges with these tough topics. The prevalence of multiple marriages and strained relationships are common. Increasingly complex financial and legal issues are typical. More people becoming self-employed and creating business assets, increasing issues surrounding privacy - all when discussed in relation to death, can become lightning rod topics. The unfortunate result can then be stalled communication and inaction.

Stress levels have been increasing, especially regarding the high number of deaths in relation to the pandemic.[14] It seems that before Covid-19, there were enough things to be concerned about. However, the general message I am suggesting you consider will help reduce your stress and enhance your overall peace of mind. There are only a few things any of us can control, but what can be managed is what we do to make our lives better. It has been proven that planning for what we want to happen as we age and exit, actually reduces the stress of growing older.[15] I realize this is not the discovery of the fountain of youth but come on - many more of you need to consider this.

What if your final wishes are not popular with your family? Comments like "just bury me in the back yard" are insensitive and short-sighted, not to mention prohibited. Most people have some familiarity with the options available after a death, but the reality is – there are now more options than ever. If, for instance, you do not want a funeral to take place after your death, your family should certainly be aware of this. However, having some sort of event to acknowledge and celebrate your life may be very important to them. Why deprive them of this? Remember, funerals are for the living – not the dead. And that is the time to have a get-together of some sort, not years after you have died. If you want your ashes to be scattered or buried somewhere other than in a cemetery, your loved ones need to know. Scattering one's ashes in a public park, as an example, though, is not recommended or typically allowed.

Men often have a more challenging time expressing their feelings. Generally, men are also less likely to seek medical advice than women.[16] Yet, it is commonly understood that regular communication with your medical advisor can save your life. I have experienced many situations where I've taken a newly widowed wife into the visitation room to see her deceased husband in the casket for the first time. (Statistically, men die at an earlier age than women).[17] Many times, these widows would say things like "he was always reluctant to see a doctor". I soon realized it was common knowledge in the industry that men generally were more hesitant to visit doctors. In several of the situations, their lack of being proactive contributed to their death.

The same concept applies to men being less inclined to discuss their final wishes. I have heard this type of comment so often – "he would never talk about what he wanted to happen after he died". The reverse, however, of husbands indicating their deceased wife never wanted to talk about such things seldom happened. I have seen this same thing play out in estate/legacy planning seminars, where the audience consisted mainly of women.

Inheritance issues can be incredibly challenging topics to discuss. Assets such as cash, investment accounts, and life insurance proceeds are easier to distribute to beneficiaries after a death. Other assets, such as vehicles, homes, cottages, businesses, etc, are much more challenging to deal with.

A growing number of estate/legacy planning specialists are recommending the concept of a family meeting during the planning process. This allows the will-maker an opportunity to explain his/her wishes to family members, describing how the estate will be distributed. Their reaction can then be considered regarding potential adjustments to the plan. Knowing the beneficiaries will likely react emotionally (especially if what they think they should be receiving is less than reality), the chances of them challenging/disputing the will after the death can be dramatically reduced. They will be more accepting of the will maker's legacy plan if they have been informed of all the details in advance, along with the reasons for setting it up that way.

It is important to note that treating children fairly regarding an inheritance does not necessarily mean treating them equally. Several factors often contribute to any decision when leaving an unequal legacy to children and grandchildren. Treating those children who have committed themselves to work in a family business is a common scenario where an unequal inheritance may be justified. Those who have provided ongoing personal care to an aging loved one is another typical scenario where this may apply. Everyone's situation is different and making sure you take the proper steps is essential.

One of the best places to start these discussions (other than with your family, of course) is with an experienced estate or financial planner. They have the skills required to help you navigate many of these issues, especially if they have earned a professional designation in estate planning. Those holding the following designations will be of the most assistance; Accredited Estate Planner (AEP), Trust and Estate Practitioner (TEP), Certified Executor Advisor (CEA), Certified Trust and Fiduciary Advisor (CTFA), Certified Financial Planner (CFP), Chartered Trust and Estate Planner (CTEP), Chartered Financial Consultant (ChFC), Chartered Life Underwriter (CLU). Trust Officers are also great resources. Mandatory continuing education requirements assure these professionals are current with industry regulations as they evolve.

Regardless of the professional advice sought out, it is fundamental to remember that a comprehensive approach is crucial. Working with a team of advisors is also highly effective because the various areas of law, taxation, and finance can all be part of a well-organized and integrated plan. Simply engaging one advisor will not lead to the most effective holistic plan. For example, financial planners often act as a quarterback in working with the other allied professionals for the client's ultimate benefit. Funeral directors, on the other hand, have typically not done so. I believe that leveraging communication and collaboration is best, especially when involved in this type of personal planning.

In my opinion, superstition holds many people back from doing what they should. Whether it pertains to investing in life insurance, discussing their funeral wishes, or the details they would like in their will. I doubt that effective communication can overcome someone's strong beliefs in that sense, but it is certainly worthwhile to try. According to the Merriam-Webster dictionary, superstition is defined as "a belief or practice resulting from ignorance, fear of the unknown, trust in magic or chance, or a false conception of causation".[18] It is easy to imagine how these feelings are very prevalent regarding death, as it is one of the great unknown realms. My great-grandmother was so superstitious that if her dinner guest list added up to thirteen, she would intentionally invite one more person to dinner; otherwise, she was convinced it was bad luck to have dinner with thirteen people. I was relatively young when my great-grandmother would do this, but apparently, she would even invite a stranger in for dinner if she had to.

While working in the funeral industry, I witnessed the effects of superstition somewhat frequently. These are not to be confused with the many different customs and traditions which are so prevalent at the time of a death. I respect the various cultural differences that exist in our society and realize they often have enormous significance.

The basis for my message is simply this; you must have a willingness to discuss these things. There is no doubt that effective communication fosters better relationships. Effective communication, therefore, is also a priority regarding end-of-life planning. Sharing your objectives through positive engagement should be the priority. Those around you will realize your desire to discuss these issues and engage with you in many cases. They may be reluctant initially, but your patience will pay off as they come to terms with your persistence. Your desire to carefully plan needs to be as strong as your love of family. Do not let procrastination get in your way. This planning is a unique gesture of love and openness for those closest to you.

You may have concerns about discussing these things with those you love. Perhaps you have attempted to talk with your family in the past, and it did not flow the way you expected. I urge you to keep this in mind. "Facing one's mortality and feeling the appropriate emotions of sadness, anger, and fear can give greater meaning to life and make it even more precious. This awareness also places one's experience in perspective and helps to avoid trivializing one's existence."[19] More people need to realize the gravity of this.

Being proactive and starting these legacy conversations is often what is needed. Your attempts may be met with replies such as "Don't talk about such things." After all, who could blame anyone for wanting to do anything other than discussing the sobering topic of death? However, accepting the fact that no one lives forever is fundamental. As Eckhart

Tolle stated, "Realize deeply that the present moment is all you will ever have". We should never assume we are too young, too healthy, or too busy to avoid dealing with our mortality. Talking with those you love about your final wishes will not result in your death occurring any sooner.

The timing of these discussions can be very delicate. It is a sensitive topic that makes many people uncomfortable and reluctant to have an in-depth conversation. Do not give up if an attempt to get the ball rolling ends with the discussion being diverted to another topic. Be patiently persistent and bring it up again when you feel the time is better. Keep in mind though, you may never find a perfect opportunity. However, the timing of news about others passing away can be leveraged to your advantage in moving your conversation forward. Many of these types of instances, such as an acquaintance becoming ill and hospitalized, can also be used as an opportunity to bring up your situation. With such an event being top of mind with loved ones, they should be more open to discussing them with you.

The questions immediately below will help you get the conversation started.

Tackling tough topics – Try these icebreakers.

A. I've been thinking more about my life and how I want to be remembered. How will you remember me?

B. If I had died last night, who do you think would be best prepared to sort everything out?

C. Did you know that planning around our eventual death reduces the stress of growing older?

D. Did you know many people die without having a will in place?

E. Do you know what happens when someone dies without a will?

Bottom line;

1.   If you die without a valid will, the government has one for you (and your wishes will be totally ignored).

2.   Consider your final wishes and communicate such with those you love while your mind is clear, and you have the opportunity.

3.   Give regular thought to the legacy you want to leave behind.

4.   Engage knowledgeable trusted advisors to obtain the most appropriate guidance for your situation.

5.   Getting your affairs in proper order will not result in your death any sooner.

# *2*

# WILL PLANNING

Having a valid will is the only way of stipulating
who you want to wrap up your life

*"Estate planning is an important and everlasting gift you can give your family. And
setting up a smooth inheritance isn't as hard as you might think."*

SUZE ORMAN, PERSONAL FINANCE EXPERT & AUTHOR

*I*n the previous section, I stressed the importance of communication. Expressing your thoughts, objectives, and concerns to the
appropriate people is fundamental. Your discussions now need to
be advanced. They cannot be left as verbal expressions only. Making sure
your objectives are appropriately recorded is a crucial next step. If your
final wishes are not properly documented, they will not be carried out.
Plain and simple. And all those other potential problems I stressed in
Chapter One due to a lack of proper planning, may haunt you and those
you love – forever.

If something is worth doing, it is worth doing right. And this certainly
applies to establishing your will. It is the solitary document in which
you can specify who you want in control of your affairs after your death.
Indicating precisely who you want as your executor is vital. Remember, if

you do not do this, government rules therefore take over. This is discussed in more detail in the following pages.

Deciding who should be in charge as the executor(s) is often a stumbling block for many people. They cannot determine who they want in charge, so they procrastinate and do not set up their will. Keep in mind you can always change who you appoint. It is not chiseled in stone. Although if you wait too long, your life could be chiseled in stone – your gravestone. Do not let your attempts to choose the perfect executor stop you from doing this. The person or persons you have in mind may not be the best fit for this role, but there is help available. There are an increasing number of resources specifically for executors to make their job easier and safer. We will be discussing executor duties and the risks in Chapter Four.

If you have not established a will, there is a good chance you have not recorded all the assets you own. This may not sound like a big deal but think about it. You are very familiar with everything which is yours – big, small and everything in between. When you are gone, no one else will be as familiar with them. Little things can mean a lot. There are many reasons why, for example, over $900 million lies dormant in unclaimed Canadian bank accounts.[20] A major one is a lack of communication! See Chapter One.

What if you die without a valid will in place? A Court office will be involved to a much greater degree. Your belongings will eventually be shared with your family members based on a default government formula. Since you opted to do nothing, the government, in essence, has a will for you. It will be based on a generic template which applies to everyone in your province, territory or state who also dies intestate. Your assets will be split up between those closest to you, but your wishes and objectives will be totally ignored. The result of you not looking after this properly is a complete lack of control on your part. You had your chance. These government intestacy rules can seem cold and unfair, but they are the only alternative for die-hard procrastinators. (Pardon the pun).

Here is what can happen if you die intestate;

- Stepchildren and, in some jurisdictions, unmarried partners may receive nothing.

- Additional administrative responsibilities will be forced onto those you love.

- Arguments within your family are much more likely to occur.

- Costly legal action may be required to work out problems.

- The ordeal could be drawn out over a much longer time (perhaps many years longer than necessary).

- Their grieving process could be more complicated.

- Stress levels forced onto those you love will be higher.

- Your legacy may become bitter and disappointing.

- And, of course, you'll be dead (trust me, it's better to die with a will).

If you have young children, this is so important. You likely have strong feelings about who you would (or not) want to raise your children if you died. Imagine that monumental decision being made by someone else, perhaps a government employee. You have died, and now someone who knows nothing of your family or personal values, is in control of making such a monumental decision. Well, it can and does happen. You may feel this is nothing to be concerned about because your surviving spouse could simply look after your children. Unfortunately, however, spouses die together somewhat frequently. Think of all the times you have traveled by car or plane together. Accidents are always happening. When I worked as a financial planner, I had several people admit they had hastily established their will just before taking a distant vacation. (These people also likely put off their studying and crammed for exams).

Here is another serious problem, which is often overlooked. When minor children in these situations become an official adult (typically at about age 18), the young and inexperienced adult can apply to the Court to have complete access to their portion of your estate. This crucial point alone deeply concerns so many people. There are several risks of a young adult coming into a sum of money. They do not have the life experience to appreciate the value of a sizable amount or how to manage it prudently. Vulnerable loved ones with access to money can easily fall prey to uncontrolled spending, manipulation, alcohol abuse, and drug addiction. For some, drug overdose and even suicide can result.

Think about that. A complete disaster could result if you do not have your affairs in proper order. And you will not be alive to turn it around. It will simply be too late. However, this is your opportunity now to step up and do it right. Do not think of the costs of being prepared as anything but a wise investment in your family. Practical legal advice does come with a price, but not being organized can be much more costly in many ways. Hiring an experienced estate planning lawyer is the very best option, especially if your situation involves family support payments, an ex-spouse, strained relationships, business interests or foreign property.

When meeting with a lawyer to establish your will, the process usually involves two or possibly three meetings. The first meeting is typically an intake session. The lawyer obtains the details required to ensure your final wishes are documented accurately and thoroughly, so they will be acceptable by a Court of law when needed. The following are the types of questions that lawyers typically ask:

- Have you discussed your final wishes with those closest to you?

- Are you wanting to do this voluntarily, or is anyone pressuring you?

- Who do you want to settle your affairs after you pass away?

- Why did you choose that person?

- Have you considered having more than one person overseeing your estate?

- Would you like to also name a backup (alternate) executor in case your first choice cannot fill the role?

- Are there any dependents who rely on you financially?

- Who do you want to raise your minor children in the event you pass away?

- Do you have an ex-spouse?

- Are there unique assets that require particular skills to manage, such as a rental property or a business?

- What is to happen if you and your spouse/partner were to die in an accident together?

- Do you have life insurance in place?

- How long do you want to financially assist/support your spouse?

- How long do you want to financially assist/support your children?

- Would you rather your children inherit a lump sum or have income provided to them over time?

- Are there any issues with beneficiaries that could be challenging, such as addiction, a disability, or strained relationships?

- Do any of your beneficiaries have any challenges with spending or money management?

- Would you want incentives included for your children, such as an additional amount paid to them upon obtaining a post-secondary diploma or degree?

- Are there particular charities close to your heart that you would like to assist financially at your death?

- Have you considered using a corporate executor?

- How do you feel about compensating your executor?

The next meeting would typically involve a detailed review of the draft will, which your lawyer prepared based on your initial appointment. Upon your agreement to the terms of the document, the will would then be signed and witnessed. Your lawyer may offer to store your will in their office for safekeeping. You will also be provided with a copy for your records and additional copies for your executor(s).

It is best if your executor(s) have a copy. Having discussed your wishes in advance with your executor(s) will also provide them with the assurance they need to fill the role. Being an executor can be complex and demanding. It is certainly not for everyone. Do not think that surprising someone and secretly naming them as your executor is a good idea. It is not. Secrecy regarding this planning tends to result in negativity and poor results.

The lawyer will also likely ask if you have a power of attorney (POA) document or personal directive in place. This document allows you to appoint an alternate decision-maker/fiduciary if you become incapacitated (i.e., unable to make decisions about your health care or finances). It is highly recommended you establish this too while engaging a lawyer for your will. Legal professionals will frequently discount their will preparation cost to include this additional information. These are discussed in Chapter Five.

A will cannot include what you want to happen in every possible future situation, but it should cover the most common scenarios. It should also provide the flexibility and control you feel is appropriate for those you are entrusting as your executor(s). This is another reason why proper legal guidance is very important.

The more information you can prepare in advance of your meeting with your lawyer, the better. This makes it easier for your lawyer and should reduce their time involvement and the resulting fee. There are an increasing number of good resources on the internet to help you prepare. There is no shortage of information, from detailed estate planning questionnaires to guidelines and articles. I highly recommend you print off a well-detailed questionnaire, complete it as best you can, and use it in conjunction with your planning. I suggest using a pencil. Providing this to your lawyer as you begin your planning is wise. Your lawyer will take the time to ensure you understand the issues regarding your situation and the rules of the jurisdiction in which you live.

Shortly after a death, the immediate family often becomes focused on finding the deceased's will. All too often, survivors do not know if there was a will established or where it can be found. This alone creates a substantial amount of unnecessary stress and frustration. Searching through the deceased's home then becomes a high priority. Knowing this vital document needs to be protected from water, fire, mold (and for those with a secrecy mentality, from prying eyes), it can lead to a wild goose chase.

If the document is suspected to be held in a lawyer's office or bank safety deposit box, that can become a significant problem. For example, if the death occurs at the beginning of a long weekend, obtaining the will can be delayed. If the deceased included their funeral wishes in the will and did not discuss these things with loved ones, it can create a timing issue.

Surviving family members often want to arrange the funeral details as soon as possible. This makes it easier to inform extended family and friends about the death and provide them with the funeral details at the same time. Family and friends who are not local need as much notice as possible to make travel arrangements so they can attend the funeral. If the immediate family is unaware of what the deceased wanted to happen, they must guess or wait until a copy of the will can be located.

A practical solution is to openly discuss your final wishes with those you care about before you pass away. Your loved ones will then know what you want to happen, and they will not be forced to guess about anything.

When you die, your original will must be accepted in a Court of law before your belongings (assets) can be distributed. The process is formally known as 'probating a will,' and it typically takes place in a Court of law where you live. The person you have named in your will as your executor is the person to look after this. You can also choose to have more than one executor. This is preferred because if your first choice is unwilling or unable to fulfill the role at the time of your death, the other can step in. Considering the timing is unknown and could potentially be decades into the future, it makes sense to include a second choice. They are often known as an alternate executor. Choosing people who are younger than yourself, is advisable.

How your will document is prepared, determines if a Court of law will accept it. If experienced legal advice has been obtained while creating it, the document will likely be acceptable. On the other hand, if no legal advice has been involved, the risk of potential problems goes up.

One of the primary reasons specific rules are in place regarding wills is to protect against forgery and fraud. If two witnesses see the will-maker (testator) sign their will, the Court has good reason to believe the will is real. Another reason for the formal process is to alert the testator to the document's importance. It is extremely serious. The testator must be mentally capable and have a good sense of the assets they own. Knowing the exact value of everything is not necessary.

Let's assume you have taken my advice. I've convinced you to discuss the fact that you won't live forever, with your loved ones. You have overcome the urge to procrastinate, gathered the inner courage, and brought up the types of questions I suggested at the end of Chapter One with them. The resulting conversations were worthwhile. It was not easy, but you did it. Congratulations. You now have a clearer idea of what you want to have happen, and so do they. You should feel proud of yourself as this process is now underway and moving in the right direction. The additional peace of mind I mentioned earlier is getting closer.

For those who have a will in place, kudos to you. Some of this information may already be familiar but considering how most people are unfamiliar with estate/legacy planning, you will likely learn something helpful. I am sure you know a few others who have been putting this planning off. Perhaps more than a few.

The use of wills dates back over 2000 years and can be traced to ancient Greece. They were used in much the same way as they are globally today, but more so back then for those who had no children or relatives.[21]

One of the most unusual wills was left by the famous magician Harry Houdini. He stipulated in his will that his surviving wife was to hold an annual séance so he could reveal himself to her. Later in his life, he became highly interested in spiritualism and séances because of the immense loss he felt for his late mother. After attempting to communicate with his dead mother through a spiritualist resulted in nothing, he gave up. In his own will, he specifically left a list of 10 randomly selected words that he said he would communicate to his surviving wife after his death. She did as her late husband requested for ten years after his death in 1926, holding a séance on each Halloween. Houdini never appeared.[22]

One of the most famous wills ever written was created here in Canada back in 1948. It was extremely brief and accepted by the Court. Cecil George Harris, a Saskatchewan farmer, carved his will into the bumper of the tractor he was pinned under. Using a small knife, he carved, "In case I die in this mess, I leave all to the wife. Cecil Geo Harris." Unfortunately for Cecil, he did not survive the incident. When the carving was discovered by one of his neighbors a few days later, the bumper was removed and brought to the Court, where it was determined to be a valid holograph will. The bumper has now achieved a sort of celebrity status in the legal community and is currently on display at the University of Saskatchewan Law Library.[23]

Holograph wills are not generally recommended, except by those wanting to avoid the cost of legal advice. Some jurisdictions, such as my home province of Ontario, allow holograph wills to be used. They must consist entirely of the testator's handwriting and be written in a specific way to avoid the person's estate from being determined as intestate. Holograph wills are not allowed in all jurisdictions.[24] However, attempting to create your own holograph will without expertise is not a good idea. As with most things in life, you get what you pay for.

There are a growing number of interactive will-maker programs available on the internet. Many of them have been created by estate lawyers and are customized to the rules of various jurisdictions. This growing trend of lawyer-approved online will services is not only convenient and cost-effective, but it has evolved from our ever-increasing do-it-yourself (DIY) society. Some of these services include various levels of legal advice, while others offer discounts toward one-on-one lawyer consultations.

The extraordinary number of deaths due to the Covid-19 pandemic resulted in many people wanting to get their wills established or updated. Virtual will planning has increased substantially, and this trend will continue. Online convenience and lower cost have proven to be very popular. However, these online providers should not be used by everyone. Below are some examples of situations where consulting one-on-one with an experienced estate lawyer will best protect you, as well as those you love:

- You are separated or divorced and have dependents who rely on you financially;

- You are being pressured to complete or update your will;

- You own property in another jurisdiction other than where you live;

- You have an ownership interest in a business;

- Your family relationships are strained;

- You have concerns about the spending habits of certain family members;

- You want to leave particular family members out of your will.

The decisions regarding your final wishes are yours to make – no one else's. If you feel pressure to establish or update your will, I highly recommend you proceed most carefully. Unfortunately, some loved ones can be forceful and may not have your best interests at heart. Those in a paid position (such as personal caregivers, for example) should certainly not be suggesting you include them in your will. Pressure in this regard is known as duress, and Courts take this very seriously. It is a conflict of interest. Many things can invalidate a will, and duress is one of them.[25]

Do not feel you have no control. Everyone has the right to make their own decisions in this way, but if you think you are under duress, I have a practical solution. Reach out to an experienced estate lawyer, not one who does wills every Tuesday morning and other legal services the rest of the week. You want a lawyer who is up to date with all the changing rules and who will provide the best value. As you meet with your lawyer, she/he will likely ask you to meet privately in their office. Anyone else except a spouse will typically be asked to wait outside the room while you speak with the lawyer privately. This is your opportunity to disclose the pressure you are feeling. Your lawyer can then work with you to resolve this important issue appropriately.

Your will should be reviewed every five years or sooner if a significant change has occurred. Some common examples are; you become a parent, get married or divorced, start a common-law relationship, your executor's situation has changed, or there are changes to the estate rules of your jurisdiction. An update would also be appropriate if you decide to add or remove any of your beneficiaries.

There you have it. Your will is now in place. Was it challenging to do? I anticipate your answer would be 'no.' It is a good feeling. I compare it to having an emotional safety net underneath me. Each time I update my will, it makes me happy knowing I am doing the best I can for those I love, regardless of what happens to me. As so well put by the famous John D. Rockefeller. "Happiness and personal fulfillment are the natural consequences of doing the right thing."

Bottom line:

1. Discuss your final wishes with your executor(s) and give them a copy of your will.

2. Online will-making services can be effective if they include legal guidance but are not for all situations.

3. If you feel pressure to complete/update your will, it may not be valid.

4. There is a long list of potential problems if you die without a will.

5. Basic fill in the blank will kits which provide no legal guidance should be avoided.

# *3*

# FUNERAL, CREMATION & BURIAL PLANNING

## Whether basic or elaborate, give your family the comfort of knowing your final wishes

*"Each of us has a responsibility to determine what is to be done with our body after we die"*

– ANONYMOUS.

One of the most challenging issues regarding death is the deep sense of loss felt by the immediate family and friends of the deceased. Witnessing these highly emotional situations is genuinely heart-wrenching. However, knowing that life continues for the survivors, the objective becomes one of assisting them toward a productive grieving process.

Losing a loved one can be incredibly difficult. Suffering this type of loss, though, is unfortunately rather common. Being able to grieve the loss in a healthy manner and continue living as a reasonably well-adjusted survivor, is crucial. Some people, however, may experience what is known as complicated grief. This can result in many symptoms such as guilt, isolation, hoarding, depression, or worse.

Experts stress the importance of specific steps that can help those in grief. The Mayo Clinic recommends, "Doing something concrete and meaningful that pays tribute to the life that was lost is one way people are often able to find closure."[26] In other words, we can help ourselves by honoring the person who has died.

The most practical way of accomplishing this is to ensure their final wishes are honored and followed in the intended manner. Whether your loved one wanted a natural green burial, water cremation, or no funeral, their wishes need to be respected. This circles back to my earlier points regarding open and effective communication. We also need to know what we want.

Knowing that you want your body to be cremated, as an example, provides your family with a unique sense of peace. They do not want to risk offending you, especially at such a delicate time. However, if they have no idea of your wishes, they can only guess. Disagreements among surviving family members are also quite common, especially after a death. Lasting regrets can linger in their minds for years, or worse, for the rest of their lives. You should not risk the chance of forcing those you love toward any form of complicated grief. It can and should be avoided. For the most part, you have that control.

When you die, your body becomes uniquely significant. It is your shell, which your family and friends are intimately familiar with. They will never have seen you in this way before. Your social identity does not disappear, at least not initially. Several decisions will need to be made by your family, and many of these decisions will be emotionally charged. Some of the decisions will also be deeply ingrained into their memory.

Your body may be discovered in an unusual place, you may need to be transported over a great distance, or you may be the focus of a forensic investigation resulting in unexpected delays. The future cannot be predicted but rest assured, delicate decisions regarding your mortal remains will need to be made. These can be uncomfortable thoughts, but from a holistic perspective, this process of proper planning will help more people than you can perhaps imagine.

We are taught from a young age that saying 'Hello' when we meet someone and 'Goodbye' when departing from their presence is the right and polite thing to do. When someone we care about dies, we have a primary and distinctive human need to say 'Goodbye'. The funeral process provides an opportunity to say that important farewell. Viewing the body of the deceased also yields other benefits:

*It provides family and friends confirmation of the death – seeing is believing.

*Viewing provides a means of social support, which can be very helpful in the mourning process.

*It provides comfort and a time for everyone to say goodbye to the deceased personally.

*It allows survivors to begin the transition into their new life, with the deceased no longer being part of it.

Whether the death resulted from natural causes or a traumatic event, I believe it is helpful (in the majority of cases) for family and friends to view the body. A healthier grieving process is then more likely to follow. Funeral directors are trained professionals who can skillfully restore a human body and create a positive outcome for that memorable and final goodbye. I have witnessed this myself many times. From the opposite perspective, if you do not want anyone to see your lifeless body, be sure to communicate this effectively.

In some cases, viewing the deceased may not be advisable. Situations involving extensive trauma, decomposition, etc, should not be viewed. Powerful medications given prior to death as an example, can make the embalming process very challenging. Embalmers certainly strive for the best possible results, but they too are only human. Morticians are not magicians. Remembering the person as he or she was, is best in such a situation.

Making the decision to have an open or closed casket can be difficult, to say the least. Usually, this decision is made by those who were closest to the deceased. If agreement cannot be reached, it may be advisable to let the majority of those closest to the deceased (majority rules) make the decision. Once decided, the extended family members and friends can then be allowed to enter the room.

Our society seems to have created an unwritten rule implying that a dead human body must be dealt with rather quickly. This is not always the case. If a loved one has been ill for some time and has chosen to die at home, the rules will likely permit the deceased to remain in the home for a while if the family prefers. This can be therapeutic for the survivors. However, if a death occurs unexpectedly and a Coroner/Medical Examiner is then involved, the rules will not likely permit any delay regardless of what the family wants. Investigations regarding the cause of death are very serious and involve the local police department.

Establishing funeral, cremation, or burial arrangements for the deceased then become a priority. Word of mouth spreads quickly about a death, and surviving family members are often eager to arrange the details so they can notify others. This step alone can make their lives easier at a most challenging time. The immediate family members closest to the deceased frequently become very busy attending to numerous things. The funeral industry stresses that there are almost one hundred decisions that may need to be attended to at the time of a death.[27] Many people plan their funeral in advance with a funeral home to make it easier for those they love—a wise decision. Prepayment is not typically required.

In the 1800s, funerals were held in the deceased's own home, as funeral homes did not yet exist. Death was much more ingrained in daily life, and perhaps death was less stressful. People were rural-living, mortality rates were higher, and most people died at home (unless a gunfight was involved). Embalming became popular in the late 1800s when formaldehyde and other similar chemicals were introduced.

A significant event that helped launch the funeral industry as we know it today was the Civil War. The need to transport bodies over large distances led to the widespread use of embalming. It became even more popular after Abraham Lincoln's embalmed body was taken on a 13-city tour after his assassination in 1865. Mourners were astonished at how well preserved he was. This was the first time Americans had seen an embalmed body, and it quickly became a national sensation.

The funeral industry has since evolved into a massive industry, with embalming being a time-honored tradition. The Funeral Consumers Alliance website explains, "Embalming is common only in the US and Canada. Many families consider it an essential part of a traditional funeral and burial arrangements, and few question whether it is necessary or what is involved in the process. It is important to remember that this perception was created by the funeral industry for commercial purposes. Most funeral directors will not arrange the public viewing of a body without embalming and cosmetic restoration."[28]

The topic of embalming has become somewhat controversial. It has been an essential service of the funeral industry for well over a century, yet it is only required in specific circumstances. If, for example, a body is to be transported outside of a province or state, embalming will be necessary. The Funeral Consumers Alliance has stated, "Funeral industry members frequently claim that dead bodies are a source of contagion to the public, and that embalming is necessary to prevent the spread of disease. Some will also claim that unembalmed dead bodies must be buried in a casket and a vault to prevent 'contamination' of groundwater. These assertions are not true."[29] Sections of this article reference opinions from the prestigious World Health Organization relating to mass fatalities and natural disasters as well.

While it is true that embalming is seldom required, the process and result do offer unique benefits. It allows family and friends the opportunity to say farewell in the most favorable environment possible. Embalming does increase the overall cost, but it is a specialized service. If a body is not embalmed, the environment nearby can become foul very quickly. This certainly does not support any type of positive environment to celebrate one's life and say goodbye.

The industry (just like many others) has been tarnished in the past. Those who have treated the dead with disrespect or have taken advantage of the bereaved and pressured them to buy products and services for financial gain are simply unacceptable. Enforcement from funeral industry regulators regarding non-compliance has increased. Providing transparent and fair pricing to consumers is held as a priority, and it should be.

Funeral regulators in Canada[30] and the United States[31] have discovered some funeral homes have not been as transparent as they should be regarding their prices. After working in the industry for years, I am confident that it is only a small percentage of funeral homes this issue pertains to. Although price disclosure and transparency are the standards, it is wise to thoroughly research before choosing a funeral provider. Consumer advocate websites can also be beneficial.

Competition is stiff in this industry. Costco and many other sources are successfully selling caskets and various funeral merchandise directly to consumers.[32] Until recently, purchasing funeral home supplies was only available through expensive specialty firms which exclusively sold to the death care industry. Now, anyone can easily buy a cremation urn, register book, or any other funeral-related item online.[33]

In my experience, few people give much thought to a death occurring away from home. There can be many obstacles to returning the deceased back home when someone dies abroad. The most straightforward option is to have the deceased cremated. The surviving family members can then bring the cremated remains home with them. Airlines will generally allow for this without any interference. However, it is essential to keep in mind that some parts of the world do not embrace and use cremation as we do here in North America. If cremation is not an option, having to return the body will be the only other alternative. Using the deceased's return flight ticket will not work.

The term used for returning a body home is known as repatriation, and it comes with a cost. I am not just referring to the high financial price but the emotional price as well. The requirements to successfully accomplish repatriation involve extensive paperwork, coordination with foreign governments, as well as health agencies. Delays are very common. Embalming is a requirement, along with precise protocols and shipping casket requirements which can vary dramatically depending upon the country. Dealing with foreign consulates and airlines regarding these matters requires specialized knowledge and plenty of patience. Language barriers and potential forensics investigations can also create additional challenges. When the heightened emotions of distraught family members are added to the situation, it can quickly become rather complex.

These issues are seldom considered when leaving for a fun-filled vacation, but unfortunately, death does not take a holiday. The unexpected loss of a loved one is hard enough to deal with on any given day. Adding all the complexities of the death occurring in another country or on another continent creates even higher amounts of stress and anxiety. Families suffering the loss of a loved one away from home cannot look after all the details of a successful repatriation. Funeral homes are familiar with these unique situations and will often have the resources/contacts to ensure all details are handled most effectively.

More funeral homes now offer cost-effective 'repatriation insurance' programs, which can provide all the services of returning a deceased to a funeral home in their home community. These are a very cost-effective and practical way of eliminating your family's risk of being in such a difficult situation. These specialized insurance programs typically include such things as locating a local licensed funeral home at the place of death (anywhere on the planet), preparation of the body for transportation, purchasing the minimally necessary shipping container, obtaining all the required documents, and transportation of the remains (including flight costs, etc) to the designated funeral home in the deceased's home community. There are generally no age or health restrictions for these forms of specialized insurance, and coverage lasts the remainder of your life.

The above form of repatriation insurance provides far greater value than what is generally available through travel agencies, employer group insurance programs, or credit card companies. These lesser quality coverages tend to have a maximum payout (a low one) and may not provide any administrative assistance. The cost of repatriation can be several thousands of dollars and will involve many hours of well-informed, high-level correspondence.

Keep in mind that if cremation is carried out in a foreign land, family and friends back home will not be able to say goodbye to the deceased in the same way as doing so with the loved one's body present. That is why I'm a firm believer in quality repatriation insurance. I have seen the comprehensive benefits of this protection so many times.

I have great respect for the entire death care industry. I've met many caring professionals who are incredibly consumer-focused and have witnessed the positive effects of countless touching funerals. I have also seen how evolving consumer demand has forced this industry to remain current and relevant.

Immediate cremation and no funeral are now much more common. Traditional funerals consisting of multiple visitation periods with an open casket followed by a church funeral and procession to a cemetery for burial, are much less common. Funeral hearses are seldom seen anymore. Society no longer views the value of a traditional funeral in the same way as in the past. Several factors have influenced this, including the do-it-yourself (DIY) evolution. Simply put, more people want to save money and be more involved.

This quote from the Huffington Post captures it well. "A growing group of Americans are returning to a more hands-on, no-frills experience of death. In the world of 'do it yourself' funerals, freezer packs are used in lieu of embalming, unvarnished wooden boxes replace ornate caskets, viewings are in living rooms, and, in some cases, burials happen in back-yards." "The reasons vary from the economic to the psychological and cultural. The average funeral costs $6,560, while a home funeral can cost close to nothing. In a society were seeing death and speaking of it is often taboo, home funeral advocates are challenging the notion that traditional funerals are anything but a natural end to life. Instead, they assert, death and mourning should be seen, smelled, touched, and experienced."[34]

The "death awareness movement" is growing for several reasons, and it was one of the motivating factors behind this book. I have been following this trend for years and have struggled to find the most appropriate way to add my voice (although I believe I have finally discovered it). Ralph White, the co-founder of the Art of Dying Institute in New York, stated, "Our initiative is a mission to reshape the understanding of death.... We consider this a reflection of American culture's growing openness to addressing death and dying more candidly."[35]

Death midwives now exist, and training programs for this relatively new role are growing in popularity. According to the End-of-Life Doula Association of Canada, "End-of-life doulas empower, educate and encourage people and their families to be involved in making decisions. The word 'doula' is Greek for servant or helper. Like a birth doula supports women during the labor process, a death doula supports a person during the dying process. This support is specific to that person's needs, beliefs, and desires. Death is a process that can span over months or even years rather than an event, and doulas can help with supporting and planning for the future, regardless of diagnosis or illness".[36]

Coffin clubs are becoming well received. Building one's own coffin (or casket as they are called here in North America) is an intriguing way of socializing with others of a similar mindset. The members' friendships and emotional bonds among themselves are the rewards of these resourceful groups. A palliative care nurse started her own club in New Zealand in 2010, and they have grown around the world since. "We think it's important that the young family members come help them to normalize the fact that people die," explained Katie Williams, founder of the first Coffin Club in New Zealand. "There's been so much 'head in the sand' thinking involved with death and dying."[37]

Another increasingly popular alternative is that of body donation to science. It is one of the fastest-growing trends among funeral alternatives and provides individuals with a practical way of supporting medical advances that will positively impact future generations' lives. Enrolling is typically done through a medical university that participates in this type of program.[38] It is important to note that there may be preliminary requirements that can preclude one from being accepted. Death from an infectious disease, recent surgery, and overall body condition is usually assessed at the time of death to determine if the body will be approved. Since many people are turning to this option, it is wise to have an alternative plan if universities are at capacity or body condition results in denial.

More people should consider being an organ donor. Almost every part of the human body can be donated, age generally does not matter, and the need for this type of gift is significant. Your medical condition will determine what organs and tissue can be used at the time of death. There is always a long list of patients needing various organs to survive.[39] You can make a gift unlike anything else to someone who desperately needs it. There is no cost, and it will be totally painless. You won't be needing your organs or tissue, so why not help someone in need? If you should decide to have an open casket for your final performance, they'll never know you stepped up to become an organ donor.

If you wish to have any part(s) of your body donated, it is essential you speak with your family about this. Otherwise, a donation may not be possible. If, for example, you mention the donation wish in your will and do not discuss this with your family, they may not be aware until it is too late. If your family/executor has your body cremated before your will is located, your donation will not occur. The same applies to your funeral wishes. Do not merely include your wishes in your will, assuming everything will somehow work out.

What if your final wishes are not popular with your family? If a tradition in your family has been burial, and you prefer cremation, how is this resolved? The answer is not black and white. However, the matter of discussing these things with your family is crucial. If you have any doubts, please refer to Chapter One – Communication is Key.

Approximately 65% of the deaths in Canada and the United States result in cremation taking place.[40] Cremation rates have been increasing for years, and this will continue.[41] A driving factor is simply cost. The price of cremation compared to burial is less, especially if your family does not already own cemetery property. Choosing cremation instead of burial also provides your family with the flexibility to determine later what is to be done with your cremated remains/ashes. Burial typically needs to take place relatively soon after a death, but cremation eliminates that urgency.

During the cremation process, much of your body evaporates. That is because you are primarily made up of water. What remains is your skeleton and ash of the casket. All metal pieces from the casket are removed, and your bones are placed in a machine that reduces them into the size of small stones. After each cremation, the chamber is cleaned to ensure that all cremated remains are thoroughly collected and packaged.

The crematorium will provide a basic container to hold your ashes unless an urn has been selected. Your ashes can be kept in the basic container and do not need to be transferred into an urn. They will not give off an odor and can be kept at home indefinitely. They do not need to be buried in a cemetery.

If you are considering earth burial (of either cremated remains or a full-size casket), it is also important to consider where your relatives are buried or will be buried. Existing cemetery property may allow for the burial of several cremated remains. Each cemetery has its regulations but burying three packages of cremated remains in one standard depth grave is not uncommon. A package of cremated remains is approximately the size of a two-slice toaster and takes up much less space compared to a full-size casket.

Purchasing a grave can be expensive. Real estate values have been increasing, and this applies to cemeteries as well. It is best to obtain a copy of the cemetery price list in advance. If you are considering the purchase of cemetery property, I highly recommend these questions be asked:

*Can you please provide us with your price list in advance?

*Can we have a tour of the cemetery?

*Is an outer container required for full-size burials?

*How many packages of cremated remains can be buried in a grave?

*What are our options if we later decide to be buried elsewhere instead?

*Are upright and flat gravestones allowed?

*Are extra depth burials allowed?

*What rules are in place regarding grave decorations (flowers)?

An outer container refers to a larger burial receptacle which holds a casket. They are commonly known as a vault or a crypt. Both are typically made of cement; however, they have significant differences. Vaults are more expensive as they provide protection from groundwater. Crypts are more basic and do not provide water protection. Both provide support for the casket and prevent the grave from settling.

Extra depth burials allow for the first burial to be deeper in the ground. Not all cemeteries offer this option, but it is worth considering if allowed. Generally, if the soil conditions of the cemetery are more of a sandy texture, extra depth burials will not be allowed. Sandy soil tends to cave in when dug to deeper depths and just isn't practical for extra depth burials.

There are an increasing number of ways to care for cremated remains than ever before. Having them placed into a cemetery niche wall is popular. Ashes can also be scattered or set into specialized jewelry or ornaments. A growing number of innovative companies are continually creating new options. Cremated remains can now be buried within an ocean reef, packaged into fireworks, or turned into a vinyl record.[42]

Traditional fire cremation has been embraced for decades and is very common. A new environment-friendly version of this is water cremation or resomation. It involves using a specific water solution to reduce the body to ash in a similar fashion to fire cremation. The significant difference, however, is much less of an environmental impact.

The funeral process is the same, but instead of the body being exposed to flame during traditional cremation, a water and alkali-based solution is used within a water chamber instead. The result is a pure white bone ash that is returned to your family as with flame cremation. As quoted by the Founder and Director of Resomation Ltd – Sandy Sullivan, "Over 135 years ago, flame cremation offered fundamental change in the way we approached human disposition and some serious convincing was required before it was fully accepted. Water cremation now offers a new, innovative yet dignified approach which uses significantly less energy and emits significantly less greenhouse gasses than flame cremation. We are once again on the cusp of revolutionising the funeral industry with the chance to provide the public with an environmental alternative at the end of life".[43] This new process is becoming increasingly available throughout Canada and the United States.

Natural green burials are increasingly popular due to society's sensitivity to climate change. The cost savings are also significant. No embalming is done, and the body is simply wrapped in a biodegradable sheet. Viewing the deceased can still be arranged but doing so should not be delayed. According to the Green Burial Society of Canada, "Green burial is a statement of personal values for those who seek to minimize their impact on the environment. For people who are mindful of the cyclical nature of life, green burial is a spiritually fulfilling alternative to conventional burial or cremation. It is an environmentally sensitive practice: the body is returned to the earth to decompose naturally and contribute to new life."[44]

So, there you have it—an undertaker's underlying thoughts about one's ultimate exit. As in life, you also have the choice about what is to happen upon your death. The key is to be proactive, think, and act in a way that supports those you love. You only have one chance to get it right.

Bottom line:

1. Give serious thought to what you want done with your body.

2. Do not risk the chance of forcing complicated grief onto those you love.

3. Realize the significance of saying 'Goodbye.'

4. Consider investing in good-quality repatriation insurance.

5. Consider becoming an organ and tissue donor.

# *4*
# ESTATE PLANNING 101

Leave a legacy, not a legal and tax headache

*"The need to leave a legacy is our spiritual need to have a sense of meaning, purpose, personal congruence, and contribution."*

— STEPHEN COVEY

*W*e all know we are going to die eventually. Those genuinely willing to plan around their death have a unique commitment to those they love and the causes they believe in. Going through the planning process often provides a rather liberating and peaceful feeling. After the planning has been initially established, the all too familiar forces of avoidance and control seem to fade.

It is natural to think of your mortality more often as you age. If you are fortunate to live to a ripe old age, these thoughts occur more frequently. Some, however, are forced to face the end of their lives sooner due to unwelcome health issues.

Facing the end of your life due to a terminal illness must be incredibly difficult. I cannot imagine it. Coming to terms with this devastating reality can be eased through a unique medically related support program known as palliative care. The World Health Organization describes palliative care as "an approach that improves the quality of life of patients (adults and children) and their families who are facing problems associated with a life-threatening illness. It prevents and relieves suffering through the early identification, correct assessment and treatment of pain and other problems, whether physical, psychosocial, or spiritual. Addressing suffering involves taking care of issues beyond physical symptoms. Palliative care uses a team approach to support patients and their caregivers. This includes addressing practical needs and providing bereavement counseling. It offers a support system to help patients live as actively as possible until death." It further states, "Palliative care is most effective when considered early in the course of the illness. Early palliative care not only improves quality of life for patients but also reduces unnecessary hospitalizations and use of health-care services."[45]

Dr. Kathryn Mannix, a well respected consultant in palliative medicine, Newcastle upon Tyne Hospitals, U.K., explains it well; "The process of dying is something we recognize and understand the sequence of. We can walk alongside of them to make sure their symptoms are well managed, as they gradually lose awareness of the world around them as their breathing slowly fades and stops."[46] Learning about palliative care often reduces or even eliminates many frightening concerns of what is often a peaceful process.

Professionals from this field are eager to improve the public's perception of this very worthwhile and unique support system. The need for palliative care is dramatically increasing. The government of Canada, as an example, has taken a bold position to expand and enhance the entire system nationwide. The Framework on Palliative Care resulted from evidence revealing Canada has fallen behind in this area. The Canada.ca website indicates, "According to the Economist Intelligence Unit's 2015 Quality of Death Index, Canada has slipped from 9th to 11th out of 80 countries based on the availability, affordability, and quality of palliative care. While the provision of palliative care has improved since its inception in the 1970s, a number of reports have identified ongoing gaps in access and quality of palliative care across the country".[47]

The number of people dying in hospital settings is declining. The prestigious Harvard Medical School reported, "Although more than 700,000 people die in hospitals each year in the U.S., the trend is toward fewer in-hospital deaths…Some of the reduction in deaths during hospital stays and emergency room visits could be due to improved treatment. But much of the decrease is probably due to other factors, including improved availability and acceptability of alternative sites of care, including hospice settings".[48]

Palliative care and hospice care are very similar. Palliative care is broad in scope and is often provided in hospital settings. On the other hand, hospice care is typically provided outside of hospital environments when someone with a terminal illness has less than six months to live. This support includes symptom relief due to the disease, counseling, help with medical equipment, and family and grief support. Curing treatment is no longer provided with hospice care.

Medical assistance in dying (MAID) is a relatively new and growing practice in my home country of Canada,[49] as well as the United States, Belgium, Colombia, and the Netherlands.[50] Although the act of intentionally bringing an end to one's life is very controversial, it is slowly becoming more accepted within our society. Ongoing debates over procedural safeguards and enhanced data collection for monitoring purposes are the tip of the iceberg regarding the highly emotional nature of this topic.

Cultural and social barriers surrounding death and dying are slowly improving. The tendency to avoid these issues out of fear is being gradually replaced by ripples of mild acceptance. Industries other than the medical field are gaining ground in convincing the public to plan around their mortality. Beyond medical care, the most prevalent areas of planning involve legal and financial guidance.

I realize everyone does not have the financial means to hire a lawyer and financial planner to assist them. However, there are an increasing number of online resources to help those who want to complete their own planning. As I have stressed earlier though, the do-it-yourself (DIY) approach does have distinct limitations. Creating your own will online as an example, is only practical if your situation does not involve such things as support payments, strained family relationships, a blended family, business or foreign property ownership, or any complex "if this then that" scenarios.

For those wanting to ensure their estate documents are thoroughly organized, engaging an experienced estate lawyer is absolutely your best option. The old adage of 'you get what you pay for,' holds very true in this sense. Legal professionals are your ultimate defense and can provide you with all kinds of relevant information, strategies, and solutions regarding such things as;

- The structing of your documents so they will be compliant with the rules of your jurisdiction.

- Practical steps to reduce the risk of your wishes being challenged or contested.

- Ways to ensure your final wishes are respected and followed.

- Advice to help you effectively decide upon the best executors for your circumstances.

- Verification that no one was influencing you before/during the preparation of your will (in case ever questioned).

- Ways to help you structure fair treatment of your beneficiaries (which does not always mean equally).

- The expectations/role of those acting as your executors.

- The common planning risks involved with such things as blended families.

- How to establish motivating financial incentives for your beneficiaries.

- Verification that you were of sound mind during the entire process (in case ever questioned).

- Information to help your executors with settling your estate.

- Strategies to help control negative emotional reactions and arguments between your beneficiaries.

- How to establish financial controls to protect any spendthrift beneficiaries (from themselves).

- Effective ways of leaving particular people out of your will (if you choose to do so).

- Help with considering everything you should when establishing your will.

- The creation of a legacy that is truly reflective of how you want to be remembered.

- Guidance to make minor changes to your will as your situation evolves.

- Their collaborative work with your financial planner and your accountant.

- The safekeeping of your original will until needed.

Yes, that is a long list, but it is important to be mindful that legal advice is vital. Attempting to accomplish estate/legacy planning without any legal guidance whatsoever is like trying to perform your own surgery. It will not be effective, and it could be just as painful. Having proper legal guidance will ensure your will is going to accomplish what you want. Ignoring this fact will result in unnecessary expenses, frustration, and stress.

Establishing a trust is something that you may also want to consider. Financial assets and other property are transferred into this legal entity for the purpose of benefiting the beneficiaries of your choosing. The primary advantage of using a trust is that it creates greater security, savings, and privacy. Trusts have been popular for hundreds of years. They can be structured in several creative ways. Trusts are certainly worth looking into, especially if your situation involves a higher net worth.

There are many details regarding the topic of wills and trusts, however, I do not want to give any impression that I am providing legal advice. I am not a lawyer. I have taken several courses in my career, including some legal information, but nowhere near the extensive training lawyers receive. I am convinced, however, that guidance from knowledgeable pro-fessionals is crucial.

In Chapter One it was pointed out that financial planners are another important part of your advisory team. They are not only crucial to the growth and protection of your money, but they often act as a quarterback with your lawyer and accountant. This type of comprehensive planning provides you and your family with the greatest peace of mind.

Financial planners who are seasoned in the area of estate/legacy plan-ning are instrumental. These planners are familiar with the current rules of your jurisdiction. They are uniquely positioned to help you with such things as:

- Strategies to help you defer or eliminate tax.

- How to arrange for timely and private transfers of money after your death.

- Ways of transferring money to your loved ones while bypassing your estate.

- Methods of creating financial security for you and those you love (short and long term).

- Ways to effectively reduce estate costs.

- Steps to create greater privacy regarding your personal affairs (i.e., Who gets what, etc.).

- Ways to help your executors with the settlement of your estate.

- How to minimize the risk for those acting as your executors.

- Cost-effective strategies to significantly benefit charitable organi-zations which may be important to you.

- Remind you to keep your estate/legacy planning current with legislative changes and your situation as it evolves.

- Ways to leverage life insurance based on your objectives.

- Strategies to help control negative emotional reactions and arguments between your beneficiaries.

- The creation of a legacy that is truly reflective of how you want to be remembered.

- Strategies to better organize your affairs.

- Determine if there are any unforeseen risks.

- Collaboratively working with your lawyer and accountant.

This detailed approach is far superior to any other method because it considers the bigger picture of your unique situation. FP Canada completed an extensive three-year survey across Canada and found those "who engage in comprehensive financial planning with a CFP (Certified Financial Planner) professional confirm significantly higher levels of financial and emotional well-being".[51] This is very compelling.

It is important to realize that some financial planners do not get involved in any estate/legacy planning. They may have a speciality focus they provide such as investment planning, retirement planning or risk management planning. These planners can provide excellent value, but it's best to ensure that you are not missing any areas. A comprehensive financial planning service is best.

Deciding upon a financial planner to work with is not always easy. One of the most effective strategies is simply to ask relatives and friends who they use (and why). Keep in mind though, a good fit for them may not also mean a good fit for you. Everyone's situation is different. I recommend interviewing three to four financial planners. This takes time and effort but is well worth it. If you're able to obtain references from existing clients, this too is valuable.

If you are not receiving professional financial planning guidance, I highly recommend you consider otherwise. There are so many benefits to working with a good financial planner. Here are just a couple; greater confidence in your future and less stress. Can you really put a dollar figure on those qualities? Investing in your future (as well as your family's future), whether you're here to enjoy it or not, is still money well spent. Your financial health is very important.

So, what is a healthy estate? It's one which has been discussed with those you love, including your executors. They respect and know what you want done. They also know how your assets (large and small) are to be distributed. Tax planning has been considered, there are no disputes, and there will be no forced asset sales to pay for unexpected taxes. Your affairs are in order. Congratulations. This is the peace of mind I have been referring to.

In many situations, family members and/or close friends are chosen as executors. Typically, this delicate decision is based on who they trust the most. If those people have acted as an executor in the past though, they should certainly be asked if they genuinely want to do it again. In my experience, most people do not want to be an executor often enough to get good at it. I'm a Certified Executor Advisor, and I would be fine with never being an executor again.

Many people provide their executor with some details of what they want for their funeral. However, very few people leave their executor with any guidance regarding the next 18 - 24 months (or longer) required to settle the estate. Most executors are forced to 'learn as they go'. This can be very time-consuming, require more legal expenses than necessary and be frustrating to the beneficiaries anxious to receive their gift from the estate.

Executors are often in a challenging position. They are always expected to keep the deceased's wishes and best interests of the estate beneficiaries a top priority, successfully handle various detailed tasks in a timely manner and maintain very good notes throughout the process. Being close to the deceased, they also need to work through their own grief simultaneously. Being an executor can be like having a very stressful part-time job for about two years.

Choosing the best people to act as your executors is not always easy. A common approach is simply to name all the adult children. This may seem like the fairest and most straightforward solution, but this strategy can easily create significant problems.

If your children already have busy lives, will they really have the required time and patience to wrap up all your affairs properly? Do they have the skills? Have they always got along, and will they be able to do so throughout the process? Remember, the time following a death (especially a parent's death) is often extremely sensitive and sometimes volatile. Emotions will likely be running high. When the sentimental aspects of dividing up your things are added to the mix, it could be a disaster waiting to happen. Brothers and sisters being forced to work together can be challenging at the best of times. It could be the worst experience ever. Expecting family harmony to continue after you are no longer alive may be unrealistic.

If there are strained relationships in your family now, they may never improve, unfortunately. Some people get to the point where they just don't care and are not open to making things right. These legacy conversations, however, can have a positive impact. Looking deep into one's soul in the context of life's meaning, is a humbling experience.

Below is a condensed list of the various duties of executors. They include, but are not limited to:

- Securing all your property.
- Communicating with all your beneficiaries.
- Locating your original will.
- Arranging your funeral/cremation/burial.
- Locating all your financial documentation.
- Completing the inventory of your assets.
- Communicating the contents of your will with your beneficiaries.
- Notifications.
- Applying for probate.

- Advertising for creditors.

- Managing and accounting for the estate.

- Completing your tax returns.

- Paying out final disbursements.

Just because you have a person in mind who is very smart and extremely organized does not always mean this is the best choice either. Adding all the work of executor to their already busy schedule may not be welcomed at all. What if the person(s) you name as your executors are unable or unwilling to be your executor at the time of your death? Remember, they cannot be forced to act in this role for you. If you choose an executor who happens to live in another jurisdiction, this too can create additional complications due to rules of the other jurisdiction needing to be followed. This deserves careful consideration.

More people should consider involving a corporate executor, at least to some degree. Many firms offer this valuable service, and yes, it does come with a cost. I will discuss that soon, but let's look at the benefits first. The Canadian Retirement Education Group Inc explains the benefits very well on their website.[52]

## "BENEFITS OF USING A TRUST COMPANY AS EXECUTOR

Experience and expertise in will and estate planning: A large portion of any trust company's operation involves acting as an executor. A trust company's staff can advise you on a regular basis in terms of coordinating the contents of your will with the other financial affairs, needs and personal changes in your life, as they are closely interrelated. In addition, planning involves determining what taxes would be payable by the estate or beneficiaries and considering procedures for minimizing or providing for these taxes.

Accessibility: A trust officer is assigned a specific estate and is personally responsible for providing customized and responsive service.

Full attention to the needs of your estate: Given the established infrastructure and continuity offered by a trust company, the operation of your estate administration is smooth. If a layperson is an executor, their attention to the executor duties could be influenced by other personal interests, age, ill health, procrastination or excessive stress due to the demands of fulfilling expectations in an area where they have no experience or expertise.

Financial responsibility and security: Most trust companies in Canada are well-established and are backed by substantial capital and reserve accounts. Trust companies strictly segregate estate assets from the general funds. They are also covered by insurance in case there is a mistake or oversight due to negligence or inadvertence.

Funding capacity: A trust company can work with the members of your family to provide for their immediate financial requirements and needs immediately after your death.

Specialized knowledge: Due to the increasingly complex nature of tax and other legislation issues relating to an estate, as well as to the wide variety of options available, a trust company employs a staff of experts to review and advise on related issues. Specialists include expertise in tax, legal, insurance, investment and other areas.

Acting as a trustee: This means that the trust company protects your ongoing interests after you die. One example would be managing your investments or capital and making payments to designated beneficiaries as required over time. If there are minor children, children from a previous marriage, or situations where the estate assets have to be controlled for an extended period of time, a trustee is required. A trustee could be giving out necessary funds from your estate over a period of 20 years or more.

Avoiding the possibility of family conflict: In any family situation there could be personality or ego conflicts, friction due to issues dealing with control, power, money, and distribution of family possessions or assets, resentment due to past financial favors to certain children or forgiveness of loans to others, unequal distribution of the estate to family members, or a multitude of other potential conflict areas. A trust company acts as a neutral, objective and professional entity in pre-empting or resolving potential disagreements affecting the administration or distribution of the estate.

Peace of mind: There is great relief in knowing that your estate will be administered competently, professionally, promptly and in accordance with your stated wishes. An experienced trust company can provide this peace of mind and feeling of security.

Finally, remember to interview a minimum of three trust companies before you decide which one is right for you."

It was mentioned above that trust companies are covered by insurance in case of a mistake, oversight, or negligence. While that is true, similar insurance can now be purchased to protect individual executors. It is a prudent step to consider especially since executors are at greater risk than ever. Estate insurance should be proactively considered in the planning process long before a death occurs.

I previously stated that an executor acts as a fiduciary. This is a high standard which requires the executor to be fully informed, timely, organized, and careful. If an executor does not act in such a manner and the estate loses money, the executor can be personally liable and sued for the loss. This is a very real risk that more people need to be aware of.

I mention the idea of engaging a corporate executor (trust company or lawyer) to suggest you may want the best of both worlds. If you decide to hire a corporate executor to work with your personally selected executor (such as a close friend), this will remove some of the heavy burdens from your friend. She/he will be able to provide your beneficiaries with the personal touch, as there is familiarity with your family. The corporate executor could look after the heavy lifting – the things which your friend would rather not do. This approach can often make good sense. Engaging a corporate executor alone may also be best, depending upon your situation.

Anyone acting as an executor has the right to be paid. While close relatives or friends may offer to do the work for no compensation, they may regret making that decision when they realize what the role really involves.

It would also not be fair to expect people to be an executor without any compensation. It is often a thankless job that some beneficiaries do not value as much as they should.

The cost of executor services can be as high as about 5% of the estate.[53] This will depend on your jurisdiction, but it can also depend upon what you arrange in advance with your executors. If your estate is well organized and will be straightforward to settle the details, the executor fee would tend to be lower. More involved estates will tend to have a higher executor fee.

Anyone asked to be an executor should know what they are getting into before accepting the role. If the will-maker (testator) has been married more than once, has strained family relationships, owns foreign property, or has been involved in a business, the executor's role will be more difficult. Knowing these types of things before the testator's death is crucial. If the testator is not taking steps to organize their estate properly, beware! This is a big red flag for anyone asked to be their executor. For the executor to have the best outcome in settling the estate, it is vital the testator plan appropriately with transparency and total engagement. If the testator is not doing this, anyone asked to be their executor should question whether they want to be involved.

Earlier, I mentioned the problem of secrecy. It is certainly understandable that issues such as infidelity or illegitimate children would cause many testators to avoid disclosure, but transparency is crucial for effective estate/legacy planning. Anything less than full engagement in this process will increase the risk of problems. Those who think they are owed something can be very forceful after a death. Consider this statement from Mondaq.com, a well-established legal information website. "The State of New York's Court system reported an approximate 350 percent increase in contested estate cases between 2016 and 2019—from 1,005 cases to 3,500 cases just three years later".[54] Do not let your estate become another bitter statistic.

Too many people do not inform those they have selected as executors that they will be an executor in the future. This makes no sense. You may like and respect someone for their strong work ethic and honesty, but this role is certainly not for everyone. Those who are named as executor should be well prepared in advance and not blindsided at the same time as being informed of the death of someone dear. The shock of, 'Surprise – you're my executor' is definitely not a responsible way of leaving a memorable legacy.

The perception of being named as executor is frequently viewed as an honor. Generally, those trusted family members who tend to be responsible, compassionate, and organized are the ones who are selected. However, the reality of being named as executor can often be very stressful unless you have plenty of free time and you think you are the best person to handle the family infighting, second-guessing, and backstabbing. Fulfilling this unique role may be the only one were you're asked to take on a major project, but you cannot ask any questions or get help from the person who asked you to take on the project.

Executors are not expected to have the knowledge of a lawyer, financial planner, or accountant. They are, however, expected always to have the testator's and beneficiaries' best interests at heart. Even a straightforward estate, though, can have issues regardless of the executor's experience or knowledge level. Beneficiaries have the right to know what is happening, but the executor is not required to consult with the beneficiaries or keep them updated every step of the way. This surprises many people.

Beneficiaries can feel that communication with the executor is an invitation for them to provide input. However, they do not have the right to offer any input, as the executors are the ones in charge. It is a prevalent yet unusual situation. Executors owe a duty of care to the beneficiaries. For example, they must keep proper records of all financial transactions and show those records to the beneficiaries if they request to see them. Executors are held to increasingly strict standards.

If you or someone you know is likely to be in the role of executor or power of attorney at some point, they should consider completing an online course which provides them with the fundamental knowledge they need. I recommend the Personal Fiduciary Certificate course through Personal Fiduciary Standards International. I recently completed this course and found it to be very good. The cost was very reasonable at

$39.95 USD. The level of difficulty was very low (beginner), a formal certificate was provided upon completion (involving a brief test), and it only took a couple of hours to finish.[55]

This type of innovative course is a great way for anyone, anywhere, to quickly become more aware of the standards they will be held to as a fiduciary. Even those who are currently in the role of executor or power of attorney would be wise to consider this type of online training.

*"The only certainties in life are death and taxes"*

− MARK TWAIN

A good amount of estate/legacy planning is tax motivated. Being proactive and planning with appropriate advice can result in substantial savings. After your death, however, the opportunity for implementing tax planning strategies is reduced drastically. The 'tax headache' in the subtitle of this chapter refers to the common regrets and frustrations which are often realized among surviving family members as the estate is settled.

A prevalent tactic is simply adding a family member as a joint owner to your bank accounts. This may seem like a logical and cost-effective idea (it generally does not cost anything), but risks are involved. The new joint owner will have access to your money, and if she/he has financial problems or a divorce, it could result in a claim on your joint account. Estate settlement involving joint accounts could be problematic if you do not adequately specify what is to happen with the account upon your death. When the one account owner dies, the surviving owner typically has complete control of the assets in the account. Joint accounts after death are a common area of estate litigation.

Payable-on-death accounts are the type that allow for named beneficiaries to be specified. Two common examples are Registered Retirement Savings Plans in Canada and 401k Retirement Plans in the United States. At the time of the account owner's death, the proceeds payable go directly/privately to the named beneficiaries specified on the account. This is a popular and straightforward strategy because the account does not form part of the estate. The more assets which form part of the estate, the higher the probate (Court) fee. Keeping the beneficiary designations on these accounts current with your wishes will allow your beneficiaries to receive money quicker than accounts included in your will. Life insurance policies also provide these same advantages.

The Investopedia website provides a good explanation of probate. "It is the process of proving the will is, in fact, the last will, and there are no challenges to it and of adjudicating any claims against the estate under Court supervision. Probate usually occurs in the appropriate Court in the state and county where the deceased permanently resided at the time of his or her death...These proceedings take time and money, and your heirs are the ones who will have to pay. Since probate proceedings can take up to a year or two, the assets are typically "frozen" until the Courts decide on the distribution of the property. Probate can easily cost from 3% to 7% or more of the total estate value".[56]

Proactive tax planning can help avoid assets from needing to be sold. If cash is not readily available to pay obligations like taxes owing, estate assets such as a cottage property or business may need to be sold quickly. A forced sale may mean the assets are sold for less than their fair value. In many cases, these things have been in the family for years. Being forced to sell a family cottage where generations of children learned to swim is something most families would prefer not to do.

After you die, the government becomes very interested in your estate. (Some would argue, too much so). In many jurisdictions throughout Canada and the United States, a greater amount of tax is forced upon estates. Planning for these things while still alive provides flexible options which are incredibly valuable. Many of those options expire when you do.

Numerous estate-related tax topics have been well covered in other books by very smart people. I am not one of them. My comments regarding tax planning are intentionally brief because this is meant to be an inspiring introduction to estate/legacy planning. I hope I am inspiring you.

Bottom line;

1. Seek out a good lawyer who focuses on estate/legacy planning.

2. Seek out a seasoned financial planner who enjoys estate/ legacy planning.

3. Choose your executors most carefully.

4. Online estate/legacy/financial planning with limited advice requires an abundance of caution.

5. Consider volunteering at a local hospice.

# 5

# POWERS OF ATTORNEY AND HEALTH CARE DIRECTIVES

Who will speak for you if you are
unable to speak for yourself?

*T*hroughout this book, it has been assumed that you can communicate with others. This section, however, relates to you no longer being able to communicate with anyone. Think about that for a moment. Not with anyone.

The Introduction mentions that avoidance and control are common feelings that many struggle with. I certainly do. I believe most people want control over their lives, although the degree to which they feel that way varies. This directly relates to the health care decisions that will need to be made for you if you become incapable of speaking. This type of situation happens frequently, and lives can quickly change forever. Taking proactive steps will remove an immense burden from those you love and, at the same time, make it much easier for the medical staff treating you. These types of situations are often very emotional. Why not do your part to make it easier? After all, this is literally all about you.

There has been no other time in recent history where Canadian and American medical professionals have had to consider the potential reality of health care services being scarce. The world was ill-prepared for the Covid-19 pandemic, and the widespread shortage of ventilators was a prime example. Doctors and nurses had to evaluate situations where they were forced to deny some patients the care they needed (therefore, they died), so others could receive care and survive. This was new territory that ran against everything these professionals were taught to do.

My typical plea before the pandemic stressed the importance of letting your closest family members know what health care services you want (or do not want) if you can no longer communicate. I have changed that approach and am now stressing the importance of getting your documents in order to make the lives of front-line workers easier as well. Front-line medical staff (and all other front-line workers, for that matter) are indeed heroes. They put in grueling long hours regularly to save lives while at the same time exposing themselves and their families to infection risk. I cannot fathom the challenges they endured during Covid-19. You have the important choice to influence doctors and nurses about your care while helping the healthcare system at the same time.

Throughout Canada and the United States, laws are in place to give people choice regarding the medical treatment they wish to receive. Unfortunately, most people have not taken steps to convey their wishes adequately. While researching this information, I discovered the Law Commission of Ontario released its final report on legal issues regarding the last stages of life. The report concludes with this bold statement; "Not enough people are planning for the last stages of life … Planning has been shown to improve patient outcomes; ensure alignment between a person's values and treatment; lessen family distress; decrease hospitalizations and admissions to critical care; and decrease unwanted investigations, inter-ventions, and treatments. Yet fewer than 1 in 5 Canadians have engaged in advance care planning".[57]

Consider this scenario. A distracted driver crashes into your vehicle, and you are left unconscious. An ambulance quickly brings you to the nearest emergency department. Your immediate family frantically arrives at the hospital to be by your side. You nor your family ever thought anything like this would happen. This sort of thing happens to other people. Not you! The hospital staff has you hooked up to several intricate machines to sustain your life. The doctors and nurses are pressing your closest next of kin for answers about what you want to be done. They don't know. Arguments break out amongst your family members over the health care they each feel you should receive. They cannot agree—tension and stress result in frustration and delays. From the hospital staff's perspective, they have seen this all too often, unfortunately.

I can relate to this scenario. Earlier, I mentioned that my mother had broken her hip, was promptly hospitalized, and died a short time later. When she flat lined in front of me and subsequently was put on life-support, we were all shocked at how fast it happened. The reality of this happening within my own family, really hit home. Fortunately, my mother had completed a power of attorney. My father, sister, and I agreed with her medical treatment, and the Court system was not required to sort out our situation. I cannot imagine how difficult it would have been to involve a lawyer and a Court office at that time. Dealing with a very sick loved one is certainly challenging enough.

Considering all that front-line medical professionals were forced to deal with (unprecedented burnout rates being just one of them), it is unimaginable that doctors were also faced with choosing one patient's life literally over another. An article in the National Post stated, "Since the novel coronavirus was first confirmed in Canada, officials in several provinces have been developing guides so that doctors don't feel alone in making life and death decisions."[58] The extremely high-stress levels resulted in many health care workers deciding to leave their jobs.[59] We all need to do our part in helping these people while at the same time – helping those we care about most, our family.

Medical care during the pandemic was frequently not as effective as it should have been, and the issue of unnecessary delays was a significant problem. Medical professionals have joined lawyers and financial planners in urging the public to have their health care wishes properly documented.

Dr. Sarah Norris, who heads palliative care at the Children's Hospital of Montefiore in New York, stresses this point so well, "When a patient first arrives, I ask them who they would want to speak for them if they are unable to speak for themselves." She goes on to say, "However, about 1 in 4 Covid-19 patients at her hospital suffer from such severe breathing issues they cannot answer. We all need to sit back and think about how someone can respect our life and maintain our personal set of values in the hospital when we are provided with care." The article continues, "Very few Americans have these estate-planning documents. Only about 23% of U.S. adults have a will, and just 6% have an advanced healthcare directive, according to the 2020 estate-planning survey by Caring.com.".. ."Doctors say this is especially true for many Covid-19 patients. There are a group of people who come in unable to complete a full sentence and can't think clearly because they haven't had enough oxygen for a while. It's important to speak at home because your last chance might not be in the emergency room".[60]

The statistics regarding end-of-life health care planning are actually worse than those surrounding will planning. The American Bar Association references a 2014 landmark study completed by the Institute of Medicine, noting, "Most people nearing the end of life are not physically, mentally, or cognitively able to make their own decisions about care. Approximately 40 percent of adult medical inpatients, 44-69 percent of nursing home residents, and 70 percent of older adults facing treatment decisions are incapable of making those decisions themselves".[61] The pandemic worsened this issue because far greater numbers of people needed urgent medical treatment.

Those who suffer from terminal health problems may not want life-sustaining medical technologies such as transplantation, feeding tubes, or ventilators used. Some in this unfortunate situation view this planning as a way of protecting themselves against technological interference that prolongs the dying process. They would rather die gently and naturally. Their quality of life is much more important to them than their quantity of life. Properly documenting their wishes provides them with that ultimate control.

Becoming incapacitated can happen to any of us at any time, for any number of reasons. Accidents and changes in health can occur very quickly, regardless of age or current situation. When doctors and nurses are forced to deal with indecision and heightened emotions of family members when the patient cannot speak, many of the problems indicated above present themselves.

Across Canada and the United States, the document which officially specifies your wishes and who is to speak for you is known as a power of attorney (POA). The word 'power' refers to the authority you give to another person(s). You are the 'donor' giving that power. The term 'attorney' refers to the person(s) you trust to speak on your behalf. In this sense, attorney does not mean a lawyer. It is important to note; the POA document is only valid while you are alive. It expires when you do.

The various provinces, territories, and states have rules that spell out what this document needs to be valid. They differ to some degree but have similarities. The document will be known as an advance care directive, personal directive, or health care proxy in some jurisdictions. In other areas, the term living will may be used (although this does seem counter-intuitive – if a will only applies after death, why such a name?).

Choosing the right person to speak for you can be difficult. That person should know you exceptionally well and respect your wishes even if they disagree. They should be willing to talk with you about your wishes, ready to come to your side in a hospital, and be prepared to speak up for you even if it is difficult. Emotions can run very high when someone is urgently hospitalized, especially when also incapacitated. The person you choose will be acting as your 'fiduciary.' This term will sound familiar because I have discussed this earlier concerning your will, in Chapter Two. Whether in life or death, the representatives/fiduciaries you select are always to act in your best interests. They are your advocate, your lifeline.

A similar document allows you to choose someone to look after your property if you become incapacitated. The fiduciary you chose for this purpose does not have to be the same as the one for your health care decisions. Your bills, as an example, will still need to be paid if you are in a hospital.

The Canadian Bankers Association specifies that a power of attorney can be:

- "for property and finances, or for health purposes,

- general (allows the attorney to act for you in any legal or financial situation) or specific (allows the attorney to act only for one transaction, e.g. sale of your house),

- limited or unlimited (e.g., limited to day-to-day banking transactions or unlimited for any financial or legal transactions),

- for a defined term or open-ended (may be limited to the time period you are out of the country/in hospital, or going forward indefinitely from the time the POA is signed),

- continuing/enduring or not (continuing/enduring refers to being in effect after you are incapable of handling your own affairs; with a non-continuing/enduring POA, the authority stops when you are no longer capable)".[62]

These incapacity documents (regardless of the name used) are extremely powerful. The person(s) you chose to act on your behalf must be carefully considered. He/she should be very trustworthy, knowledgeable, and able to handle your affairs appropriately. They should also have the time available, adequate financial management skills, and be able to keep accurate financial records. Fiduciaries need to be fair, transparent, and organized. Anything less will likely lead to complications and potential legal problems.

Fiduciaries are held to a high standard, and if they act inappropriately, they can face harsh Court penalties. The following are typical expectations they must abide by;

- to use reasonable care in all their actions

- to always be fair, transparent, and not secretly profit

- to maintain good records and be willing to account for all decisions

- to consult the donor as often as possible

- to not allow their personal interests to conflict with that of the donor

- to personally manage their authority (cannot delegate responsibly unless the document allows such)

Just as with estate/legacy planning, having proper legal guidance when establishing these incapacity documents is very important. There are also a growing number of online sources which can be used to set these up. When doing so, it is vital to ensure your wishes will be compliant with the rules of the jurisdiction where you reside. Engaging an experienced lawyer to guide you through this process (along with your will planning) is the best way of ensuring your wishes will be respected.

A lawyer is not always required, however. Nor is typically registering these documents with any organization or authority. This results in very little oversight from any Court unless a problem or concern develops. Incapacity documents regarding property (especially financial issues) are, therefore, unfortunately, very prone to abuse. There are ways, though, to reduce these risks.

The very best way is to carefully select who you choose in the first place. Having two fiduciaries making decisions together can also be an effective way of reducing the risk of abuse. It is highly recommended that these documents be reviewed with your fiduciaries every year or two. This open communication will help ensure those who speak for you will understand your wishes well. It is relatively common for a donor to choose the same fiduciary to speak for them while alive and also after their death (as their executor). There is nothing wrong with this. It may be a better approach than involving too many people, which some may not be a good fit for the role. Choosing the most appropriate people to represent you if incapacity should strike and then also to settle your estate can often be the most prudent approach. They know you and your situation well.

Another effective way to help reduce the risk of financial abuse is to notify the financial institutions you deal with that you have established a power of attorney. By providing them with a copy of your document, you will be able to confirm they will accept and honor it. This also allows you to ask that you (or someone else you trust) be notified regarding any sign of potential abuse. Some financial institutions will only accept their documents, so this needs to be clarified before any incapacity occurs. Also, they may only accept relatively current documents.

As with will planning, it is best to name an alternate fiduciary here too. If your primary fiduciary is unable or unwilling to act for you, having a backup is best. Otherwise, the Courts will likely need to get involved. Keeping the Courts out of your planning while you maintain control is more time-efficient, less costly, less stressful, and much better for everyone's sanity.

If anyone urges you to establish a power of attorney, you have a right to be suspicious. This is especially true if such applies to your finances. Just as with will planning, the issue of undue influence can result in your documents being invalid. Anyone who can benefit from these completed documents needs to be very cautious. Courts take this issue seriously. On the other hand, your immediate family members suggesting this as a group out of sincere concern is quite different. Your best interests should always be the number one priority.

Keeping your wishes up to date has several benefits. Among other things (which I have stressed throughout this book), it will help you avoid the following type of situation. A good friend of mine shared his recent frustrations about his elderly widowed father being urgently hospitalized due to a broken hip. My friend, an only child and fiduciary for his father, could not pay his father's bills for a long time because the lawyer's office was unwilling to release his father's power of attorney document. His father's older document stated some very unusual wording that caused numerous problems, especially in conjunction with the Covid-19 pandemic. I realize a widespread infectious outbreak could not have been anticipated, but more open communication and transparency in advance would have made the situation so much easier.

Some feel that simply adding a person they trust to their bank account is wise. Adding your son or daughter as a joint account owner would seem to make sense, as he or she could pay your bills if you become incapacitated. It looks like the simplest solution, but is it? If your child happens to get divorced, your account could be jeopardized by your child's ex-partner. You will have less control of the account and could even be hit with an unexpected tax bill. If your child happens to be sued or has financial difficulties such as bankruptcy, your account could be at risk. If you happen to die, your other children (or relatives) may fight over your account, especially if it was not clear what you wanted to be done with it.[63] I realize this point was discussed in the previous chapter, but it also applies here.

Dr. Richard Shulman of the Capacity Clinic in Toronto explains that two questions are used to determine mental capacity.

1.  "Is the person able to understand information relevant to making the decision; and"

2.  "Is the person able to appreciate the consequences of a decision or lack of a decision?"[64]

Completing these documents while you can do so is vital. Once mental capacity is diminished, this planning can no longer be completed. It is then too late. (Does this sound familiar?) Establishing your power of attorney before it is needed is so much better than doing nothing. Ignorance is not bliss. Those who do not correctly plan in this way may be forcing those they love to deal with government authorities such as the Public Guardian and the Courts. This is not a responsible approach.

Thinking about our potential incapacity is not uplifting, but considering the risks of doing nothing, it is important. Well-known celebrities are not immune either; they just attract media coverage. The famous Los Angeles Disc Jockey – Casey Kasem, had his share of problems after being diagnosed with dementia. His children from a previous marriage took their stepmother to Court over allegations that she isolated their father from his family and friends.[65] Supporting those fundamental relationships is crucial for looking after someone else's best interests, especially when they are suffering from mental capacity issues. The co-creator of Marvel Comics, Stan Lee, also had problems surrounding power of attorney issues before his death.[66] You may not have the high net worth and status of a celebrity, but these issues are happening all the time. Money seems to make the problems worse.

Those you choose to act as your power of attorney fiduciaries need good ethical character traits. If you become incapable, they need to respect and fully understand that your relationships with others still need to be maintained. Just because they are not fond of certain relatives of yours does not mean they can keep you from them. Previous marriage situations come to mind. Their feelings must be set aside in favor of you, the donor.

Just as with estate/legacy planning, your health care wishes should be discussed openly with those closest to you. Having a family meeting to discuss your preferences concerning who will be in charge and why you chose them can be very helpful. If your family members know the reasoning for your choices, they will be more likely to understand and support your decisions. The fiduciaries you choose do not have to be family members. In some cases, choosing a close friend (or two) may make more sense. In other cases, a corporate fiduciary may be best.

Fiduciaries are generally entitled to be compensated, but in terms of powers of attorney, they often fill the role without expecting to be paid for it. The person(s) you ask to be responsible for your property (including all your financial assets) will likely find this rather demanding. Providing compensation should certainly be considered. If you wish to compensate your fiduciaries, speaking with your lawyer about properly arranging for this within your documents is advisable. If you decide to use a corporate fiduciary (such as a Trust Company or lawyer), be aware they will charge for this service. Depending upon your situation, though, it may well be worth it. Compensation for your power of attorney fiduciaries will be similar to that regarding your executors (and based on your jurisdiction, of course). Compensation must always be viewed as reasonable, especially in the eyes of a judge.

If you are asked to be a fiduciary under a power of attorney, you should be cautious. Obtaining independent legal advice before agreeing may also be wise (depending upon the complexity of the situation). Many asked people are not aware of all the expectations they are to abide by. There are few resources to turn to for help in this unique role, yet it can be a highly criticized position at the same time. Standing up for the donor's health care wishes can be challenging, especially when the donor requires urgent health care.

Being responsible for the donor's finances and property can be extremely sensitive. Other family members (and even close friends) will likely be watching closely. As a fiduciary, you always want to be in a position of strength by being able to explain all decisions you make on behalf of the donor. Maintaining detailed notes and a time log to indicate time spent on various tasks is also prudent.

If you have accepted the role of fiduciary for someone, there are things that you are not allowed to do. Typically, you cannot;

1.  Make a will for the donor.

2.  Change the donor's existing will.

3.  Name or change any of the donor's beneficiaries on any of their registered savings plans or life insurance policies.

4.  Delegate any of your responsibilities to anyone else unless the donor indicated otherwise in the POA document.

Determining mental capacity usually involves two physicians, each completing an independent assessment. I have included the stipulation within my own power of attorney that if my mental capacity is ever questioned (other than my wife's opinion, which I don't think should count), I want a professional capacity assessor to provide one of the assessments. A capacity assessor is a specialist in determining precise levels of cognitive abilities. Considering the increasingly stretched medical resources, I do not want to rely on two emergency room doctors who are run off their feet to quickly determine my mental status. I will have to live with the consequences, not them.

BOTTOM LINE:

- Think deeply about the health care services you would want, or not want.

- Ask someone you trust to speak for you, if you can no longer do so yourself.

- If one already has dementia, it will be challenging to establish a valid POA.

- Do not keep your original POA in a bank safety deposit box, as the original may need to be shown to open the box.

- Keep your original POA safe and mark copies clearly.

- Your family and your health care providers will very much appreciate your thoughtfulness.

- Do not procrastinate with this planning.

- This important process will enhance your relationships and reduce your stress.

- You need to have your affairs in order.

- This planning will likely make you happier.

- Share this book with others you care about.

# SUMMARY

*I*f you take these suggestions to heart, your situation will be better in several ways. The hardest part of this whole process is having the courage to discuss these things with those you love. These discussions though, support everything else. The following quote summarizes my thoughts well. "Death – along with taxes – is one of life's few certainties. Despite this inevitability, most people dread thinking and talking about when, how or under what conditions they might die. They don't want to broach the topic with family, either, for fear of upsetting them. Ironically, though, talking about death 'early and often' can be the greatest gift to bestow on loved ones".[67]

One of the most common concerns many people have about their death, is worrying about abandoning those they love. Concern for their short and long term well being is top of mind. Financial resources (especially if limited) are often a significant worry.

After many years working as a Certified Financial Planner, as well as in the role of licensed funeral director, I can honestly say the best guidance I can provide to ease these concerns, is for you to leverage the advice within this message. Everything I have shared is based on real life experience and is not exaggerated.

Proactive planning is much more challenging to complete when an unwelcome health issue is also in the equation. Effective planning involves several decisions, and it certainly requires a clear mind. Investing any remaining time into the loving relationships of your life needs to be the highest priority, while turmoil is not distracting everyone, especially you.

If you are diagnosed with a severe health issue, you will be extremely relieved you took the time to properly plan when times were good. Having that peace of mind while also dealing with poor health is a true blessing. If your death is swift and unexpected, your family will be very relieved that you were so thoughtful, loving, and kind.

As stressed in the Introduction, there is no reason to put this important planning off any longer. Don't become overwhelmed with the details of what is involved. Take one step at a time, and don't be afraid to lean on others who are familiar with these topics. Type 'end of life planning reduces stress' into any online search engine and read up on all the benefits. Talk about these things with those you love and learn about your options. Live with an attitude of gratitude and enjoy your life.

# GLOSSARY

401k Retirement Plan. "A tax-advantaged retirement account offered by employers in the US". Lusk, Veneta. "What to Know About 401(k)s — the Investment Vehicles That Can Help You to Save for Retirement." Business Insider. Last modified September 3, 2021. https://www.businessinsider.com/what-is-401k.

Accredited Estate Planner (AEP). A professional designation earned by successfully completing the rigorous educational requirements set by the National Association of Estate Planners & Councils in the United States.

Adjudicating. Acting as a judge. "To make an official decision about who is right in (a dispute)". "Definition of ADJUDICATING." Dictionary by Merriam-Webster: America's Most-trusted Online Dictionary. Accessed January 15, 2022. https://www.merriam-webster.com/dictionary/adjudicating.

Alkaline Hydrolysis. A process that uses water and potash lye within a special pressurized tank to reduce human remains to bone and biological fluid. Another alternative to traditional fire cremation which results in a similar type of ash that is returned to the family for final disposition. Also known as 'Resomation' or 'Water cremation'. See 'Dissolution', 'Disposition of human remains'.

Alternate decision maker. A person specifically named to make decisions for oneself. Often used regarding incapacity. See 'Delegate', 'Fiduciary', 'Health care directive'.

Beneficiary designation. The specifying of a person (or more than one) to benefit from property of the deceased such as an investment account or life insurance policy upon the owner's/insured's death. Proceeds are typically paid directly and privately to the beneficiary thereby avoiding inclusion in the estate and the resulting probate fees. See 'Private asset transfer'.

*C*

Canadian Institute of Certified Executor Advisors (CICEA). The leading organization dedicated to educating and supporting those who serve executors.

Certified Executor Advisor (CEA). A professional designation earned by successfully completing the rigorous educational requirements set by the Canadian Institute of Certified Executor Advisors (CICEA).

Certified Financial Planner (CFP). A professional designation earned by successfully completing the rigorous educational requirements set by FP Canada.

Certified Trust and Fiduciary Advisor (CTFA). A professional designation earned by successfully completing the rigorous educational requirements set by the American Bankers Association (ABA).

Chartered Financial Consultant (ChFC). A professional designation earned by successfully completing the rigorous educational requirements set by the Financial Industry Regulatory Authority (FINRA) in the United States. This designation was previously available in Canada and has since been grandfathered for those who attained it beforehand.

Chartered Life Underwriter (CLU). A professional designation earned by successfully completing the rigorous educational requirements set by The Financial Advisors Association of Canada. (Also known as Advocis).

Chartered Trust and Estate Planner (CTEP). A professional designation earned by successfully completing the rigorous educational requirements set by the American Academy of Financial Management.

Coffin club. A social club organized with the focus of members building their own coffin for future use. The concept began in New Zealand. The term coffin is more frequently used outside North America and refers to a burial container being wider at the shoulders. The North American term is casket, which is not wider at the shoulders.

Compliance. "That all rules and requirements have been met". "Definition of COMPLIANCE • Law Dictionary • TheLaw.com." The Law Dictionary. Last modified July 12, 2014. https://dictionary.thelaw.com/compliance/.

Complicated grief. "Painful emotions are so long lasting and severe that you have trouble recovering from the loss and resuming your own life". "Complicated Grief - Symptoms and Causes." Mayo Clinic. Last modified June 19, 2021. https://www.mayoclinic.org/diseases-conditions/complicated-grief/symptoms-causes/syc-20360374. Also known as persistent complex bereavement disorder.

Consumer advocate website. Informs and educates consumers from an unbiased perspective regarding marketplace issues without the agenda of trying to sell something.

Contested estates. The final affairs of a deceased person which are formally objected against concerning the deceased's will being questioned as valid.

Corporate executor. The business entity named by a will maker to carry out the instructions within one's will. See 'Trust company'.

Cosmetic restoration. The process of restoring human remains to a similar state as when alive. Professional embalmers/funeral directors are skilled in this art and use such things as specialized make-up and wax.

Cremation. The mechanical, thermal, or other dissolution process which reduces a human body into bone fragments. See 'Alkaline hydrolysis', 'Fire cremation', 'Resomation', 'Water cremation'.

Crematorium. An establishment (often located within cemetery property) where human remains are cremated.

Death doula. A trained and supportive person who assists patients, family, and friends during the dying process. The term 'doula' is Greek and refers to someone who is a helper—also known as a death midwife.

Death awareness movement. A way of thinking which argues the cultural censorship of death is short-sighted and unhealthy.

Decedent. A person who died.

Delegate. A person who has been appointed as one's personal representative. See 'Alternate decision maker', 'Fiduciary', 'Incapacitated'.

Designated investment beneficiaries. The named individuals who are to receive the monies from an investment account after the account owner's death. See 'Estate bypass', 'Private asset transfer'.

Designated life insurance beneficiaries. The named individuals who are to receive the payout after the death of the life which was insured under the life insurance contract. See 'Estate bypass', 'Estate liquidity', 'Private asset transfer'.

Designation. A professional certification that demonstrates one's attained education level within a particular area of study and includes the right to use a title and letters after one's name which represents the designation awarded by the certifying entity.

Disgruntled heir. A person who feels entitled to receive more money or property from an estate.

Dissolution. The process of breaking down human remains into their component parts. See 'Alkaline hydrolysis', 'Human composting', 'Resomation', 'Water cremation'.

Disposition of assets. Giving up possession of items owned as the result of one's death.

Disposition of human remains. The process of dealing with a dead human body.

Duress. Forcing someone (selfishly) to do something such as establishing their will or power of attorney documents. If duress can be proven, the applicable documents will be deemed as invalid by a Court of law. See 'Contested estates', 'Undue influence'.

Estate administration. "Estate administration is the process by which an individual's lifetime financial affairs are wound up and their property and assets are distributed after they die". "What is Estate Administration?" The American College of Trust and Estate Counsel. Accessed January 15, 2022. https://www.actec.org/estate-planning/what-is-estate-administration/. See 'Estate settlement'.

Estate administrator. The person or company in charge of settling the deceased person's estate who died without a valid will. Appointment is by a Court of law to fulfill this role. See 'Intestate'.

Estate bypass. Leveraging beneficiary designations to legitimately avoid the typical requirement of having to pay probate fees. Bypassing the estate allows beneficiaries to receive their inheritance sooner (and privately) versus being included within the estate. See 'Designated investment beneficiaries', 'Designated life insurance beneficiaries', 'Private asset transfer'.

Estate costs. A local Court office will often be involved with an estate regard-less of whether the deceased had a valid will. Court offices charge a probate fee, and the fee depends upon the rules of the applicable jurisdiction. The executor settling the estate is also entitled to be compensated (and if such is a professional executor a fee will be charged). If legal services are required, the overall estate costs will be higher. See 'Corporate executor'.

Estate liquidator. The term used for executor in the province of Quebec, Canada.

Estate liquidity. The cash available in an estate, or assets which can be quickly turned into cash.

Estate planning. "Estate planning is the process of arranging for an orderly transfer of your assets to the people you want to receive them". "Estate Planning Explained." GetSmarterAboutMoney.ca. Last modified April 9, 2020. https://www.getsmarteraboutmoney.ca/plan-manage/plan-ning-basics/wills-estate-planning/estate-planning-explained/. See 'Legacy planning', 'Mortality mindset', 'Pre-need funeral planning', 'Private asset transfer', 'Tax planning'.

Estate settlement. Another term for 'Estate administration'.

Estate trustee. Another term for 'Executor' or 'Executrix'.

Exclusion clause. Specific wording in a will which intentionally leaves particular people out. See 'Contested estates', 'Disgruntled heir'.

Executor. The person(s) named by a will maker (testator) to carry out the wishes within their will and settle the estate. See 'Fiduciary', 'Personally liable'.

Execute a will. The act of carrying out the wishes contained within a valid will after the will maker has died.

Executrix. The term for a female executor.

Extra depth burial. Refers to the first burial being further in the ground, to allow for a second burial above it.

Fiduciary. A person or organization which acts on behalf of another with a duty to always keep the other person's best interests as the highest priority. See 'Alternate decision maker', 'Executor', 'Certified Executor Advisor', 'Certified Financial Planner', 'Certified Trust and Fiduciary Advisor', 'Chartered Financial Consultant', 'Chartered Life Underwriter', 'Power of attorney', 'Trust and Estate Practitioner', 'Trust company', 'Trustee', 'Trust Officer'.

Fire cremation. Dating back to the Roman and Viking cultures thousands of years ago, the practice of burning the dead has been a prevalent method of disposition. Modern fire cremation occurs in large retort ovens that operate between 1,400- and 1,800-degrees Fahrenheit. A growing number of other options are becoming available. See 'Resomation', 'Human composting', 'Water cremation'.

Forensic investigation. A thorough and detailed analysis completed by a medical examiner regarding the cause of death. The findings are often used to determine who is at fault and gather recommendations to improve public safety and prevent deaths in similar situations. See 'Medical examiner', 'Post-mortem investigation'.

Forgery. The act of falsely making or altering a document, such as a will or power of attorney.

Fraud. The act of deceiving others.

Funeral. The gathering of family and friends to celebrate a life lived. Such can be elaborate or basic but should reflect the values and beliefs of the deceased.

Funeral celebrant. A qualified person who works with a family to conduct an appropriate send-off, customized to the values and wishes of a deceased person and the immediate family. Such a person may or may not also be a funeral director.

Green burial. A form of burial that supports a reduction of the environmental impact on the earth. The elements typically permitted must be biodegradable including the casket and clothing. Embalming, burial crypts, and burial vaults are prohibited. Also known as natural burial. See 'Outer container'.

## H

Houdini, Harry. One of the most famous magicians of all time. Born in 1874 in Budapest, Hungary and died in 1926 in Detroit, Michigan.

Health care directive. A document used to specify one's health care wishes in advance, often in conjunction with the naming of someone to speak on one's behalf if need be. See 'Alternate decision maker', 'Delegate', 'Power of attorney', 'Power of attorney donor'.

Holistic. Relating to the completeness of estate/legacy planning to ensure one's legacy will be as memorable as the life lived.

Holograph will. The simplest form of a will which is typically written strictly in the handwriting of the will maker. Not all jurisdictions allow these types of wills to be used. See 'Testator'.

Hospice. A facility that provides support to the terminally ill in a homelike environment to maintain the best quality of life possible. Family members are frequently active in the care of their dying loved one.

Human composting. "The world's first human composting facility will let us recycle ourselves. In life, we strive to reduce and reuse. The human composting center Recompose aims to offer a more sustainable death". Smith, Lilly. "The World's First Human Composting Facility Will Let Us Recycle Ourselves." Fast Company. Last modified November 26, 2019. https://www.fastcompany.com/90434525/the-worlds-first-human-composting-facility-could-help-us-recycle-ourselves. See 'Dissolution'.

Incapacitated. When someone is no longer able to function normally, such as after a serious change in health.

Inheritance. Money or objects one receives after the death of the person who gives it.

Inquest. The official process to determine the cause of someone's death. See 'Forensic investigation', 'Medical Examiner', 'Post-mortem investigation'.

Intestate. The unfortunate situation where one dies without having a valid will in place. See 'Procrastinators'.

Joint owner. An individual or entity that is officially on record as owner, along with at least one other joint owner.

Jurisdiction. The territory over which authority is exercised. As an example, Canada consists of several provinces and territories, each being a distinct jurisdiction.

## L

Legacies. Gifts provided to others through their will (and/or a trust) after they die. See 'Trusts'.

Legacy planning. Organizing one's affairs to help ensure their memory in the minds of survivors is lovingly positive for the longest time possible. Contributing to charitable causes may also be important.

Legislative changes. The making and passing of new laws.

Liabilities. Financial obligations which one is to yet repay, even in death.

# $\mathcal{M}$

Mass fatalities. Situations involving more deaths than can be sufficiently managed by local medical examiner/forensics teams.

Mausoleum. A large building (usually on cemetery property) used for the purpose of above ground burials, in individual spaces known as tombs. When a deceased is buried in a mausoleum they are said to be entombed.

Medical assistance in dying (MAID). "The administering by a physician or nurse practitioner of a substance to a person, at their request, that causes their death; or the prescribing or providing by a physician or nurse practitioner of a substance to a person at their request, so that they may self-administer the substance and in doing so cause their own death". "Medical Assistance in Dying." Ministry of Health and Long-Term Care / Ministère De La Santé Et Des Soins De Longue Durée. Last modified May 13, 2021. https://www.health.gov.on.ca/en/pro/programs/maid/. Strict rules surround this process, which became legal in Canada in 2016 and at the time of writing, was legal in several American jurisdictions. See 'Quality of life'.

Medical examiner. Another term for Coroner.

Mentally capable. Having "sufficient understanding and memory to comprehend in a general way the situation in which one finds oneself and the nature, purpose, and consequence of any act or transaction into which one proposes to enter". "Medical Definition of MENTAL CAPACITY." Dictionary by Merriam-Webster: America's Most-trusted Online Dictionary. Accessed January 15, 2022. https://www.merriam-webster.com/medical/mental%20capacity. See 'Incapacitated'.

Morgue. A place or establishment used to store human remains awaiting identification, post-mortem examination, and final disposition. Medical examiner's offices and hospitals often contain a morgue.

Mortality mindset. The awareness of life's delicate nature and a grateful appreciation for every day one has.

Mortality rate. The number of deaths within a specific population of people over a given time frame.

Mourning process. According to the Kubler-Ross model, denial, anger, bargaining, depression, and acceptance are the most common reactions to loss.

Net worth. The difference between the assets and liabilities of an individual or company.

Niche wall. A structure specifically designed to hold cremated remains individually. They are often built as walls containing many plaques of deceased's names and are usually located on cemetery property.

Notarial will. "Is drawn up by a notary and is made in the presence of a witness provided by the notary. A second witness is required in some cases (for example, when the testator is blind). The will must be drawn up in French or in English, as you wish, and must indicate the date and place where it was made". "Notarial Will." Ministère De La Justice. Accessed January 15, 2022. https://www.justice.gouv.qc.ca/en/ your-money-and-your-possessions/wills/forms-of-will/notarial-will/.

Organ donor. A person who has registered to be part of their local organ donation program, permitting in advance for a donation of organs and/or tissue to be made at the time of their death. Everyone is a potential donor regardless of medical condition or age. One person's selfless gift can save up to eight lives and improve the lives of over seventy other people. The need is significant. See 'Death awareness movement', 'Legacy planning', 'Mortality mindset', 'Transplantation'.

Outer container. The term used in the funeral industry typically referring to a burial crypt or vault. These containers hold the casket and provide additional protection.

Palliative care. Medical and related care for those who suffer from serious, life-threatening illness to manage symptoms and improve the quality of life for the patient. See 'Hospice'.

Personally liable. Being legally responsible for something.

Post-mortem examination. Another term for autopsy.

Power of attorney. A legal document used to give formal permission for another person to act on one's behalf. See 'Alternate decision maker', 'Delegate', 'Fiduciary', 'Health care directive'.

Power of attorney donor. The person giving the formal permission for another to act on their behalf.

Pre-need funeral planning. The process of arranging for one's end-of-life wishes, before one's death. Depending on personal preference, a funeral ceremony may or may not be included.

Private asset transfer. The process of using/leveraging the efficiency of beneficiary designations to allow for the (after death) private and prompt transfer of money to those people, one wants to receive it. See 'Designated investment beneficiaries', 'Designated life insurance beneficiaries', 'Estate bypass', 'Tax planning', 'Trusts'.

Probate. "The administration of an estate in which the decedent either had or did not have a will". "Probate Definition: 101 Samples." Law Insider. Accessed January 20, 2022. https://www.lawinsider.com/diction-ary/probate. See 'Estate costs'.

Procrastinators. Those who typically say things like 'I'll get around to it' and frequently put off what should be done. See 'Intestate'.

## Q

Quality of life. One's level of happiness in relation to being healthy, comfortable, and engaged.

## R

Registered Retirement Savings Plan (RRSP). A popular Canadian savings plan which provides tax benefits while saving for retirement. See 'Designated investment beneficiaries', 'Estate bypass', 'Estate liquidity', 'Estate planning', 'Tax planning'.

Repatriation. The process of returning a deceased person to their home community from where the death occurred. See 'Pre-need funeral planning'.

Repatriation insurance. A specific form of insurance which covers the costs (and often all the arrangement details) of returning a deceased traveler back to a funeral home in their home community, from anywhere. Many funeral homes in Canada sell such insurance.

Resomation. A process which uses water and potash lye within a special pressurized tank to reduce human remains to bone and biological fluid. Another alternative to traditional fire cremation which results in a similar type of ash that is returned to the family for final disposition. Also known as 'Alkaline Hydrolysis' or 'Water cremation'.

Restitution order. An order issued by a Court of law to pay money to a victim of a criminal offence.

## S

Social identity. The aspect of the deceased maintaining their persona in the minds of nearby survivors for a period of time immediately after their death.

Spendthrift beneficiary. One who is often unable to control their spending habits concerning an inheritance.

Tax planning. The analysis of one's financial situation in conjunction with leveraging appropriate strategies to legitimately reduce taxation for oneself and loved ones. See '401k Retirement Plan', 'Designated investment beneficiaries', 'Designated life insurance beneficiaries', 'Estate liquidity', 'Estate planning', 'Legislative changes', 'Liabilities', 'Registered Retirement Savings Plan', 'Trusts'.

Testator. One who makes a will for themself.

Transfer service. A basic end-of-life service which typically provides transportation and arrangement for cremations and burials, for those who do not require visitation or formal funeral services. Also known as a funeral home alternative.

Transplantation. "A surgical procedure in which tissue or an organ is transferred from one area of a person's body to another area, or from one person (the donor) to another person (the recipient)". "NCI Dictionary of Cancer Terms." National Cancer Institute. Accessed January 20, 2022. https://www.cancer.gov/publications/dictionaries/cancer-terms/def/transplantation.

Traumatic event. A situation that causes damage to a human body.

Tribute. The act of paying final respects to a loved one by honoring and completing their final wishes.

Trust and Estate Practitioner (TEP). A professional designation earned by successfully completing the rigorous educational requirements set by the Society of Trust and Estate Practitioners.

Trust company. "A corporation legally authorized to serve as executor or administrator of decedents' estates, as guardian of the property of incompetents, and as trustee under deeds of trust, trust agreements, and wills, as well as to act in many circumstances as an agent. Trust companies may have commercial banking departments, and commercial banks may have trust departments". "Trust Company." Encyclopedia Britannica. Accessed January 20, 2022. https://www.britannica.com/topic/trust-company. See 'Corporate Executor', 'Fiduciary'.

Trust officer. "Offer clients trust-related services at a trust company, bank, or investment management firm and are often the primary point person for trust clients and their advisers. They administer and manage trust accounts and ensure account administration complies with federal and state laws. They handle individual and business accounts and sometimes oversee aspects of large or corporate trusts, including calculating disbursements or preparing appropriate tax forms. They may also be involved in investment decisions and trust execution". "What Does a Trust Officer Do? Role & Responsibilities." Glassdoor Job Search | You Deserve a Job That Loves You Back. Accessed January 20, 2022. https://www.glassdoor.ca/Career/trust-officer-career_KO0,13.htm.

Trusts. "A trust is traditionally used for minimizing estate taxes and can offer other benefits as part of a well-crafted estate plan. A trust is a fiduciary arrangement that allows a third party, or trustee, to hold assets on behalf of a beneficiary or beneficiaries. Trusts can be arranged in many ways and can specify exactly how and when the assets pass to the beneficiaries. Since trusts usually avoid probate, your beneficiaries may gain access to these assets more quickly than they might to assets that are transferred using a will. Additionally, if it is an irrevocable trust, it may not be considered part of the taxable estate, so fewer taxes may be due upon your death. Assets in a trust may also be able to pass outside of probate, saving time, court fees, and potentially reducing estate taxes as well". "What Is A Trust? - Fidelity." Fidelity Investments - Retirement Plans, Investing, Brokerage, Wealth Management, Financial Planning and Advice, Online Trading. Accessed January 20, 2022. https://www.fidelity.com/life-events/estate-planning/trusts. See 'Estate bypass', 'Legacy planning', 'Private asset transfer', 'Spendthrift beneficiary', 'Tax planning'.

## U

Undue Influence. "A judicially created defense to transactions that have been imposed upon weak and vulnerable persons that allows the transactions to be set aside. Virtually any act of persuasion that over-comes the free will and judgment of another, including exhortations, importunings, insinuations, flattery, trickery, and deception, may amount to undue influence". "Undue Influence." TheFreeDictionary.com. Accessed January 20, 2022. https://legal-dictionary.thefreedictionary.com/undue+influence. See 'Contested estates', 'Disgruntled heir', 'Duress'.

Urn. A container used to hold the cremated remains of a deceased person. Such may be elaborate or very basic. Urns are often made from wood, metal or ceramic materials and come in various shapes.

## W

Wake. A term used in the past relating to mourners keeping watch over the deceased until burial in case the person should wake up. The term used today throughout North America is visitation, which relates to a time of providing emotional support for the immediately family of the deceased.

Water cremation. A process which uses water and potash lye within a special pressurized tank to reduce human remains to bone and biological fluid. Another alternative to traditional fire cremation which results in a similar type of ash that is returned to the family for final disposition. Also known as 'Alkaline Hydrolysis' or 'Resomation'.

# ACKNOWLEDGEMENTS

To my dear wife, Shari Barnsdale, your love and patience have been a blessing.

My esteemed father, Jim Barnsdale, I could not ask for a bigger fan.

My late mother, Margaret Barnsdale, I am sorry you did not live to see the completion of this achievement. Love you forever.

My stepdaughter Sam Hancock, your support and creativity have been greatly appreciated.

My mentors; David Chilton, Richard McCaw, Mark O'Farrell, David Barnsdale, David Garvie, Doug Tardif, Jim Reger, John Hill, and Barry Siskind. Your insight and wisdom have been inspiring.

My key volunteer book testers (in no particular order); Penny Holden, Louise Doyle, Sharon Craigen, Diane Sutherland, Peggy Halligan-Rodman, Wendy Warren-Timpano, Danette Lefaivre, Valerie Krausse, Jim McMullen, Greg Barnsdale (of Michigan), Chaplain Nathaniel Scobie, Wendy Tarasoff, Sheila Radmann, Dianne Wakelin, Ramona West, Larry Busch, Kristin McCosh-Bagshaw, Bev Fraser-Redden, Lou Pedron, Angela Melchior, Sheila Armstrong, Michelle Ewbank-Theriault, Linea Patterson, Paul Tremeer, Darlene Burtch, Alex Rattray, and Gerry Lodwick. Without your support and ongoing thoughtful feedback, this book would certainly not be what it is today.

## ACKNOWLEDGEMENTS

To all those special people I have met in the financial, funeral, and legal industries who have made a distinct impression upon me.

For those who regularly have the uncomfortable conversations with others about death and incapacity, I empathize with you. Tackling these tough topics is not easy but necessary.

To myself, for persevering with this unconventional mission, which sums up my life's work. Though it has taken many years to write this book, I am very proud of the final result.

All of you have helped me in one way or another, and for that, I am eternally grateful.

Thank you.

# RESOURCES

*I* have a great list of resources that will help you learn more about a variety of topics covered in this book, and then some. I've even included a few sources who offer dissenting opinions, but don't listen to them. Plus there is a section that covers consultants and suppliers that may be of help to you.

However, because I'm constantly finding fantastic new material and people, it made sense to move this list online where I can update it regularly. Visit it anytime at www.DoNotIgnoreYourMortality.com There is no registration or password needed. I think you'll be impressed. Other readers stop by often and have frequently made excellent suggestions for me to check out and potentially add.

# CITATIONS

## Chapter One

1.  "Deaths in Canada 2020." Statista. Last modified September 29, 2020. https://www.statista.com/statistics/443061/number-of-deaths-in-canada/.

2.  "Number of Deaths in the United States Today As of August 2, 2021 at 2:21:21 PM." IndexMundi – Country Facts. Accessed August 2, 2021. https://www.indexmundi.com/clocks/indicator/deaths/united-states.

3.  Worldometer. Accessed August 2, 2021. https://www.worldometers.info/.

4.  "What 'will' Happen with Your Assets? Half of Canadian Adults Say They Don't Have a Last Will and Testament." Angus Reid Institute. Last modified February 1, 2018. https://angusreid.org/will-and-testament/.

5.  Gallup. "Majority in U.S. Do Not Have a Will." Gallup.com. Last modified May 18, 2016. https://news.gallup.com/poll/191651/majority-not.aspx.

6.  STEP. Accessed August 12, 2021. https://www.step.org/system/files/2020-05/estate_planning_in_australia_final_report_021017v_2_051017.pdf.

7.  "Fewer People in the UK Have Wills in Place Than Last Year, with Nearly Four in Ten over 55s Having No Will at All." Unbiased.

co.uk. Last modified September 26, 2016. https://www.unbiased.co.uk/pro/press-releases/fewer-people-in-the-uk-have-wills-in-place-than-last-year-with-nearly-four-in-ten-over-55s-having-no-will-at-all-26-9-2016.

8.  Gardner, Hannah, and USA TODAY. "USA TODAY." USA TODAY. Last modified January 2, 2017. https://www.usatoday.com/story/news/world/2017/01/02/chinese-wills-savings-beijing/95750124/.

9.  Forbes. Accessed August 12, 2021. https://www.forbes.com/sites/maggiegermano/2019/02/15/despite-their-priorities-nearly-half-of-americans-over-55-still-dont-have-a-will/?sh=39ade0455238.

10. "Ontario to Spend $72 Million to Tackle Courts Backlog, Hire Court Staff." CBC. Last modified October 29, 2021. https://www.cbc.ca/news/canada/toronto/ontario-court-backlog-1.6229951#.

11. "Legal Definition of ESTATE PLANNING." Dictionary by Merriam-Webster: America's Most-trusted Online Dictionary. Accessed August 15, 2021. https://www.merriam-webster.com/legal/estate%20planning.

12. Randall, Steve. "Most Canadians Are "dangerously Underinsured" Report Warns." Financial Advice, Planning News & Resources | Wealth Professional. Last modified October 30, 2019. https://www.wealthprofessional.ca/news/industry-news/most-canadians-are-dangerously-underinsured-report-warns/321403.

13. "How Much Time Does It Take to Settle an Estate?" Seniors and Boomers Services Alliance. Last modified May 27, 2013. https://seniorsboomersservicesalliance.wordpress.com/2013/05/27/how-much-time-does-it-take-to-settle-an-estate/.

14. "APA: U.S. Adults Report Highest Stress Level Since Early Days of the COVID-19 Pandemic." Https://www.apa.org. Last modified February 2, 2021. https://www.apa.org/news/press/releases/2021/02/adults-stress-pandemic.

15. "Article: End-of-Life Planning Can Ease the Stress of Getting Older, Experts Say." The John A. Hartford Foundation. Accessed August 15, 2021. https://www.johnahartford.org/dissemination-center/view/article-end-of-life-planning-can-ease-the-stress-of-getting-older.

16. "Why Are Men Less Likely Than Women To Seek Medical Care." Complete Wellbeing. Last modified December 28, 2020. https://www.completewellbeing.ca/men-medical-care/.

17. "Life Expectancy by Country and in the World (2021)." Worldometer - Real Time World Statistics. Accessed August 15, 2021. https://www.worldometers.info/demographics/life-expectancy/.

18. "Definition of SUPERSTITION." Dictionary by Merriam-Webster: America's Most-trusted Online Dictionary. Accessed September 12, 2021. https://www.merriam-webster.com/dictionary/superstition.

19. "Life-Affirming Death Awareness." Psychology Today. Last modified March 26, 2010. https://www.psychologytoday.com/ca/blog/the-human-experience/201003/life-affirming-death-awareness.

## Chapter Two

20. "Unclaimed Balances." Bank of Canada. Accessed September 12, 2021. https://www.bankofcanada.ca/unclaimed-balances/.

21. Hicks, Patrick. "The History of the Last Will and Testament." Trust & Will. Last modified October 16, 2020. https://trustandwill.com/learn/history-of-last-will-and-testament.

22. Brunobanana. "10 Unusual Last Wills And Testaments." Listverse. Last modified May 7, 2020. https://listverse.com/2008/08/23/10-unusual-last-wills-and-testaments/.

23. Brown, Jessica. "Dying Saskatchewan Farmer's Will Goes Down in History | Globalnews.ca." Global News. Last

modified October 25, 2013. https://globalnews.ca/news/926746/
dying-sk-farmers-will-goes-down-in-history/.

24. "Holographic Will Definition." Investopedia. Last modified
November 18, 2008. https://www.investopedia.com/terms/h/
holographic-will.asp.

25. "Undue Influence in Estate Planning." Www.nolo.com. Last modified May 25, 2012. https://www.nolo.com/legal-encyclopedia/
undue-influence.html.

## Chapter Three

26. "Complicated Grief – Symptoms and Causes." Mayo Clinic.
Last modified June 19, 2021. https://www.mayoclinic.org/
diseases-conditions/complicated-grief/symptoms-causes/
syc-20360374.

27. "Free Download: 87 Things to Do After Someone Dies." Funeral,
Cemetery & Cremation Services | Arbor Memorial Inc. Accessed
September 25, 2021. https://www.arbormemorial.ca/en/
start-planning/resources/87-things-to-do-after-someone-dies.

28. "Embalming Explained, Answers to Frequently
Asked Questions." Funeral Consumers Alliance.
Last modified December 2, 2020. https://funerals.
org/?consumers=embalming-what-you-should-know.

29. "Dead Bodies and Disease: The "Danger" That Doesn't Exist."
Funeral Consumers Alliance. Last modified May 11, 2016. https://
funerals.org/?consumers=dead-bodies-disease-danger-doesnt-exist.

30. "Registrar's Directive: Price List Disclosure on
Websites." Bereavement Authority of Ontario.
Last modified August 20, 2021. https://thebao.ca/
registrars-directive-price-list-disclosure-on-websites/.

31. Gibson, William E. "Some Funeral Homes Don't Disclose Required
Pricing." AARP. Last modified April 20, 2018. https://www.aarp.

org/home-family/friends-family/info-2018/ftc-funeral-home-pricing.html.

32. "Caskets: Search Result." Costco. Accessed September 25, 2021. https://www.costco.ca/CatalogSearch?dept=All&keyword=caskets

33. "Funeral Supplies: Search Result." Electronics, Cars, Fashion, Collectibles & More | EBay. Last modified March 24, 1041. https://www.ebay.ca/sch/i.html?_nkw=funeral+supplies.

34. "Dealing With Death: The Growing Home Funeral Movement." HuffPost. Last modified December 7, 2017. https://www.huffpost.com/entry/home-funerals-death-mortician_n_2534934.

35. Booth, Stephanie. "The Death Positive Movement Is Changing Lives." Healthline. Accessed September 25, 2021. https://www.healthline.com/health-news/the-death-positive-movement#Death-as-a-positive-mindset.

36. "Helping People Live". Accessed September 25, 2021. https://endoflifedoulaassociation.org/.

37. Booth, Stephanie. "The Death Positive Movement Is Changing Lives." Healthline. Accessed September 25, 2021. https://www.healthline.com/health-news/the-death-positive-movement#Death-as-a-community-builder-.

38. "Donating a Body to Science for Medical Research in Canada." Canadian Funerals Online. Last modified June 4, 2021. https://canadianfunerals.com/donating-a-body-to-science-for-medical-research-in-canada/#.YjzBBX167-J.

39. "Facts About Organ Donation | UNOS Organ Donor Facts." UNOS. Last modified June 30, 2021. https://unos.org/transplant/facts/.

40. "U.S. Cremation Rate 2019." Statista. Last modified June 10, 2020. https://www.statista.com/statistics/251702/cremation-rate-in-the-united-states/.

41. "Canadian Cremation Rate 2000-2020." Statista. Last modified June 2, 2021. https://www.statista.com/statistics/916310/cremation-rate-in-canada/.

42. "Top 10 New Funeral Trends." TalkDeath. Last modified December 18, 2020. https://www.talkdeath.com/top-new-funeral-trends/.

43. "A Need For Change." Resomation. Last modified August 6, 2019. https://resomation.com/about/a-need-for-change/.

44. "What is Green Burial — Green Burial Society of Canada." Green Burial Society of Canada. Accessed October 5, 2021. https://www.greenburialcanada.ca/greenburial.

## Chapter Four

45. "Palliative Care." WHO | World Health Organization. Last modified August 5, 2020. https://www.who.int/news-room/fact-sheets/detail/palliative-care.

46. "What is Death Like?" The Art of Dying Well. Last modified December 3, 2019. https://www.artofdyingwell.org/what-is-dying-well/our-journey-through-life/what-is-death-like/.

47. Health Canada. "Framework on Palliative Care in Canada." Canada.ca. Last modified July 12, 2019. https://www.canada.ca/en/health-canada/services/health-care-system/reports-publications/palliative-care/framework-palliative-care-canada.html.

48. "Where People Die." Harvard Health. Last modified October 31, 2018. https://www.health.harvard.edu/blog/where-people-die-2018103115278#.

49. Health Canada. "Second Annual Report on Medical Assistance in Dying in Canada 2020." Canada.ca. Last modified June 30, 2021. https://www.canada.ca/en/health-canada/services/medical-assistance-dying/annual-report-2020.html.

50. "Chronology of Assisted Dying in the U.S." Death With Dignity. Last modified May 21, 2021. https://deathwithdignity.org/learn/ assisted-dying-chronology/.

51. FP Canada. Accessed November 10, 2022. https://fpcanada.ca/ docs/default-source/communications/value-study.pdf.

52. "BENEFITS OF USING A TRUST COMPANY AS EXECUTOR | Estate Planning." Www.snowbird.ca | Everything Canadians Need to Know About Enjoying the Snowbird Lifestyle. Last modified July 19, 2006. https://www.snowbird.ca/2006/07/19/ benefits-of-using-a-trust-company-as-executor/.

53. "Paying Your Executor." GetSmarterAboutMoney.ca. Last modified June 19, 2017. https://www.getsmarteraboutmoney. ca/plan-manage/planning-basics/wills-estate-planning/ paying-your-executor/.

54. "Estate, Trust And Fiduciary Litigation Will Continue To Grow - Family and Matrimonial - United States." Welcome to Mondaq. Last modified August 5, 2021. https://www.mondaq. com/unitedstates/wills-intestacy-estate-planning/1099268/ estate-trust-and-fiduciary-litigation-will-continue-to-grow-.

55. "PFSI." PFSI. Accessed November 10, 2022. https://thepfsi.com/ en/home.

56. "Avoiding Unnecessary Probate Costs." Investopedia. Last modified December 2, 2004. https://www.investopedia.com/ articles/04/121304.asp.

## Chapter Five

57. "Hull & Hull LLP." Hull & Hull LLP. Accessed October 12, 2021.

58. "How Doctors in Canada Will Decide Who Lives and Dies if Pandemic Worsens." Nationalpost. Last modified April 3, 2020. https://nationalpost.com/pmn/news-pmn/

canada-news-pmn/how-doctors-in-canada-will-decide-who-lives-and-dies-if-pandemic-worsens.

59. "Ontario Health-care Workers Warn of 'brutal' Nurse Shortage As Hospitals Brace for 4th Wave | CBC News." CBC. Last modified September 14, 2021. https://www.cbc.ca/news/canada/toronto/ontario-health-care-workers-warn-of-brutal-nurse-shortage-as-hospitals-brace-for-4th-wave-1.6150255.

60. Epperson, Sharon. "As Coronavirus Continues to Spread, Doctors Urge Americans to Get a Living Will." CNBC. Accessed October 12, 2021. https://www.cnbc.com/2020/04/27/as-coronavirus-continues-doctors-urge-consumers-to-get-living-will.html.

61. "If There is No Advance Directive or Guardian, Who Makes Medical Treatment Choices?" American Bar Association. Accessed October 12, 2021. https://www.americanbar.org/groups/law_aging/publications/bifocal/vol_37/issue_1_october2015/hospitalist_focus_group/.

62. "Powers of Attorney: What Consumers Need to Know." Canadian Bankers Association. Accessed October 31, 2021. https://cba.ca/powers-of-attorney-what-consumers-need-to-know.

63. "If You're Thinking of Putting Assets into Joint Ownership with Your Children, Read This First." Financialpost. Last modified January 26, 2019. https://financialpost.com/personal-finance/if-youre-thinking-of-putting-assets-into-joint-ownership-with-your-children-read-this-first.

64. "When More Help is Needed: Moving Seniors with Dementia to Care Facilities." All About Estates. Last modified August 3, 2018. https://www.allaboutestates.ca/capacity-consent-care-facilities/.

65. "Casey Kasem's Case Highlights Need for Power of Attorney, Lawyers Say | CBC News." CBC. Last modified May 15, 2014. https://www.cbc.ca/news/world/casey-kasem-s-case-highlights-need-for-power-of-attorney-lawyers-say-1.2644593.

66. Malito, Alessandra. "Stan Lee's Tangled Web of Estate Planning and How to Avoid It in Your Own Life." MarketWatch. Last modified November 17, 2018. https://www.marketwatch.com/story/stan-lees-tangled-web-of-estate-planning-and-how-to-avoid-this-mess-2018-11-14.

67. Carr, Deborah. "End-of-life Conversations Can Be Hard, but Your Loved Ones Will Thank You." The Conversation. Last modified January 10, 2022. https://theconversation.com/end-of-life-conversations-can-be-hard-but-your-loved-ones-will-thank-you-173614.

# HELP SPREAD
# THE WORD

---

*I*f you feel my message provides value, please feel free to share your thoughts on social media and by telling others. I am working hard to make a positive difference in the lives of others. Your endorsement on platforms such as Amazon and Goodreads will help me to make more of an impact. Thank you.

# ABOUT THE *Author*

Greg is an unusual undertaker.

Despite having embalmed hundreds of people during his career, he often gets queasy when giving blood.

The Canadian Red Cross has banned him. He is not to come back, ever.

Having plenty of experience as a last responder and an end-of-life advisor, he has grown increasingly frustrated with what he's witnessed.

Far too many people feel 'it won't happen to me,' and they just don't want to talk about it.

This widespread avoidance he's found over a 30-year career compelled him to write this book and share an increasingly important message. We should accept our mortality and plan to be remembered.

As a genuine disruptor and advocate for the 'death awareness movement,' he has a compelling message –

Plan while you can.

Doing so can enhance relationships, reduce stress and save you money.

He is on a mission to inspire people (with a bit of humor) to leave a legacy rather than a mess.